A new look at
Mysteries
of Archaeology

The secrets of many ancient civilizations are still locked in the past. In recent years, with the aid of modern technology and the knowledge gained from patient research, archaeologists have made a wealth of discoveries about the peoples of the past. But questions still remain. Did the lost continent of Atlantis ever exist? Are the Hanging Gardens of Babylon merely a legend or were they really built for a princess long ago? Why did the Mayans suddenly desert their vast cities?

In this beautifully illustrated book, we study 11 of the past's most elusive mysteries and explore different theories about what really happened all those years ago. Each topic begins with a vivid story, illustrated with a large, full-colour picture, telling what probably happened. This is followed by a discussion of possible solutions to the mystery, using photographic evidence and drawings of clues found on the site. Finally, there is either a game or project to bring each story alive in a practical way. Foreign words and archaeological terms (italicized) are explained in the text or in the illustrated glossary.

ARCO

Acknowledgements

Author: Michael Gibson

Adviser: Bruce Welsh, MA, Institute of Archaeology, London

Managing Editor: Trisha Pike

Editor: Jo Jones

Art Editor: Adrian Gray

Picture Researcher: Julia Calloway

Projects Adviser: Krysia Brochocka

Illustrators:
Reconstruction artwork by Roy Coombs and Steve Crisp of Artists' Partners. Project artwork by Carolyn Scrace. Other illustrations by Tom Stimpson.

Published by:

Marshall Cavendish Children's Books Limited,
58 Old Compton Street,
London W1V 5PA, England.

IN THE U.K., COMMONWEALTH AND REST OF THE WORLD, EXCEPT THE UNITED STATES OF AMERICA

Arco Publishing, Inc.,
219 Park Avenue South,
New York, N.Y. 10003, U.S.A.

IN THE UNITED STATES OF AMERICA

Library of Congress Cataloging in Publication Data

Main entry under title: A New look at mysteries of archaeology.
  Extent includes index.
  SUMMARY: Discusses eleven mysteries of the ancient world including the lost continent Atlantis and ancient Viking settlements in North America. Includes a project or game for each mystery.
  1. Archaeology – Juvenile literature.
  2. Civilization, Ancient – Juvenile literature.
  3. Antiquities – Juvenile literature.
  (1. Archaeology. 2. Civilization, Ancient.
  3. Antiquities)
  1. Arco Publishing.
CC171.N47   930   80–11383
ISBN 0–668–04956–1

ISBN 0 85685 832 3

First printing 1980
This printing 1981

Pictures

All Sport/John Starr 22B; Peter Andrews 17, 18; Barnaby's Picture Library 6–7, 11T, 75B; BBC Hulton Picture Library 16–17, 46T; Stephen Benson 40T, 64, 65BL, 75T; Courtesy of the Trustees of the British Museum 41, 42; Peter Clayton 23, 34–5, 47; Fotograf Dehlholm/Forhistorisk Museum 70–71B; Michael Dixon 11B, 71B; Les Drennan 19, 25, 31, 37, 43, 55, 67, 73; Fiore 40B, 46–47; Historisk-Arkaeologisk Forsogscenter 59; Holloway Bros. 74; Hong Kong Tourist Association 16; Iraqi Cultural Centre 35; Mansell Collection 22T; Marion Morrison 65BR; Tony Morrison 65T, 66; Ian Murphy 52, 53T & C, 54; Nationalmuseet, Copenhagen 71; Parks, Canada 70; Ann & Bury Peerless 28, 29; Courtesy of Queen Victoria Museum, Zimbabwe-Rhodesia 53B; Royal Danish Ministry for Foreign Affairs 58; Ronald Sheridan 10; Vorderasiatisches Museum, Berlin 34; West Air Photography 24; Yale University Press 70–71T.

Contents

Secrets of the Past   6
The Lost Empire   8
Atlantis   10
Search for the City   12
Giants and Men   14
Dragons' Bones   16
Make a Giant Jaw-bone   18
A Temple to the Sun   20
Stonehenge   22
Reconstruct the Past   24
The Attack   26
The Indus Civilization   28
Make an Indus Ox-cart   30
The Prophecy   32
The Hanging Gardens of Babylon   34
A Miniature Garden   36
The Great Rebellion   38
The Maya   40
Paint a Mayan Folding Book   42

The Minotaur   44
The Palace of Knossos   46
Mazes and Labyrinths   48
King Solomon's Mines   50
Great Zimbabwe   52
Build an Ancient Settlement   54
The Sacrifice   56
The Peat Bog Murder Mystery   58
Solve a Murder   60
The Nazca   62
Lines in the Desert   64
Design Your Own Nazca Drawing   66
Vinland   68
The Vikings in America   70
How to Make a Viking Hall   72
More Unsolved Mysteries   74
Glossary   76
Index   78

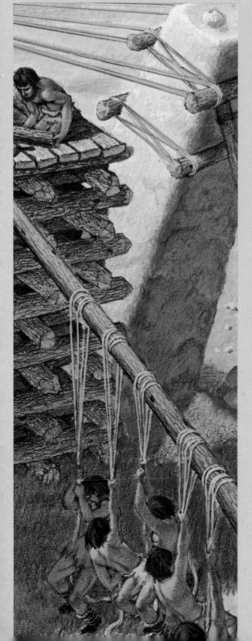

Secrets of the Past

One of the loneliest places in the world is Easter Island in Polynesia. South America lies 2500 miles to the east and Pitcairn Island 1200 miles over to the west. Easter Island is famous for its statues, the 'Eyeless Watchers'. There are 600 standing stones varying from one metre to 12 metres in height. In the island's quarries archaeologists have found incomplete monsters some 22 metres in length. The statues, which have enormous heads and tiny, squat bodies, seem to be staring hard at some invisible object in the far distance.

How and when did settlers come to this remote and desolate little island, whose total area is only 18 hectares? What can archaeologists do to answer such questions when there are no written records and only a few *artefacts* (man-made objects) to go on? In the past such problems were usually 'solved' by experts who argued that the ruins were the relics of an ancient *civilization* introduced by some advanced race from elsewhere.

Thor Heyerdahl, the Norwegian archaeologist, has been one of the most enthusiastic believers in this kind of theory. In 1947, he and five companions sailed a raft made of *balsa-wood* logs from Peru 4300 miles across the Pacific Ocean to the Polynesian Islands. He believes that civilized Europeans made their way across the Atlantic to Peru and started a civilization there, and that the Peruvians, in their turn, crossed the Pacific and colonized the Polynesian Islands centuries ago. Heyerdahl has succeeded in showing that Peruvians could have sailed to the Polynesian Islands, but he has not proved that they did.

Early visitors to Easter Island could not understand how such 'primitive' people as the Polynesians could have raised the heavy statues themselves. Yet, during a later visit by Heyerdahl to Easter Island, islanders managed to lift one of the huge fallen statues without the use of modern tools after only 18 days' hard work. Having lifted one end of the stone by pushing timbers under it, they gradually levered the stone upright by raising it a few centimetres at a time and propped it up with a supporting wall made of stones. Slowly but surely the stone was moved towards an upright position. The final stage was accomplished with ropes. It seems evident, therefore, that there is no technical reason why these 'primitive' people should not have constructed and lifted all the statues themselves.

A much more difficult question to answer is: why did these islanders spend so much of their time and energy on these apparently useless activities? In fact, all over the world, early peoples seem to have spent a great deal of time on similar pursuits such as drawing elaborate lines in the desert and building huge and complex temples to their gods. It may be that these time-consuming occupations helped the rulers keep their people under control. In other words, we have no definite answers to most of these questions.

The rest of the stories in this book come from all over the world and show how *prehistoric* or early peoples accomplished the most astonishing feats. The study of *archaeology* is filled with mysteries. Many have been unravelled, still more remain to be solved. Sometimes ancient ruins yield up their secrets to the careful researcher, often they only provide tantalizing snippets of information. Frequently archaeologists are left with nothing but their intelligence and imagination to help them.

As you read this book, see if the explanations that are offered seem logical and correct. Can you think of any other explanations? If you can, try to work them out clearly.

Left: These 'Eyeless Watchers' have been guarding Easter Island for hundreds of years.

The Lost Empire

Our founder and first king was Poseidon, God of the Sea. The great god married a mortal woman called Clito who bore him five pairs of twin sons. The first-born, Atlas, gave his name to our great empire, Atlantis. Poseidon and his descendants turned our land into a paradise upon Earth, and extended our rule over many of the lands of Europe as far as Italy and Egypt.

Atlantis was rich not only in agricultural produce but in minerals, metals and timber. Its forests were full of all kinds of animals and the plains were feeding grounds for huge elephants. Our capital city was built on a mighty hill. On its summit, we built a *citadel* containing a magnificent palace which was regarded as one of the wonders of the world. In the middle of the citadel lay our masterpiece, the temple of Poseidon and Clito. Inside, we gathered all that was valuable including gold, silver, precious jewels and ivory. The chamber was dominated by a colossal statue of Poseidon driving a team of six winged horses, surrounded by sea-nymphs riding on dolphins.

The circular citadel was surrounded by a huge moat. Outside this, there were two circles of land separated by a second moat. On these circles were built magnificent horse-racing stadiums, splendid gardens, gymnasiums and fine temples. The outer ring of land was encircled by a third even wider moat where merchant ships from all over the world lay at anchor. This final moat was protected from the sea by a wall. All three moats were connected by a canal so that ships could sail from the sea through an opening in the wall directly to the capital city.

The city lay close to the sea at the edge of a wide plain which contained deep lakes and sparkling rivers and was protected by a range of mountains.

Our laws were the envy of our neighbours. They were engraved on an enormous bronze pillar in the temple of Poseidon. Every five years, our under-kings gathered here to try important cases. But before they could do this they had to perform an ancient ritual. According to the sacred law, the under-kings had to capture and sacrifice a wild bull using only wooden staves and rope. Once the bull had been sacrificed, there were great celebrations. As soon as these were over, the under-kings put on their deep-blue robes and sat in judgement on all cases brought before them.

Unfortunately, as time went by, my people became more and more spoilt and the gods grew tired of our pride and decided to punish us. They went to Poseidon and called on him to punish us. Sadly, the great god agreed.

The following day dawned fine and warm. Then, towards noon, huge black clouds appeared and, in a little time, the sun was hidden from sight. In the murk, great flashes of forked lightning split the clouds, thunder rumbled and then an enormous explosion was heard. Out at sea, a huge volcano rose up above the waves, casting out molten lava in all directions. As we sailors watched horrified from our ship, the sea began to boil and a huge *tidal wave* rushed towards Atlantis.

What happened then, neither I nor my companions can tell you, because we spent the next few days fighting for our lives while our little ship was battered by mountainous seas. When the storm eventually died down, we sailed back to where our home had been. But there was nothing left except some wreckage floating in the water. Of the beautiful land of Atlantis there was no sign. It and its inhabitants had disappeared off the face of the Earth, as if they had never been.

Right: The people of Atlantis flee from an enormous tidal wave which destroys everything in its path.

Atlantis

Above: These are some of the places which have been put forward as the site of Atlantis.

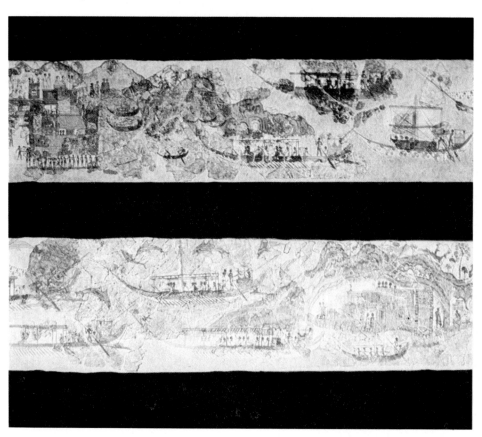

Above: This fresco was found on the island of Santorini. It may show invaders who helped destroy the Minoan civilization.

The story of Atlantis has fascinated people for 2500 years. Where did the story come from? The answer is simple. Plato, the famous Greek philosopher, wrote two *dialogues*, the *Timaeus*, and the *Critias*, which contain conversations between Plato's old teacher, Socrates, and some of his friends. During these discussions, the story of Atlantis is told. The story was not mentioned by any writer before Plato's day and many experts believe that it is nothing more than a flight of the great philosopher's imagination.

Nevertheless, generations of people have found the idea of a lost continent absorbing. During the Middle Ages, the story was almost forgotten, but during the Age of Discovery, with the voyages of Christopher Columbus to America and Vasco da Gama to India, interest in Atlantis revived. However, the story did not really interest scientists until Paul Schliemann, the grandson of Heinrich Schliemann, the famous archaeologist who *excavated* Troy, wrote an article in 1912 called *How I discovered Atlantis, the Source of all Civilization*. Schliemann claimed that his grandfather had left him an envelope containing all the information he had about Atlantis recounting how, during his

10

work at Troy, he had come across a superb bronze bowl inscribed, *From King Chronos of Atlantis*.

As a result of this article, and in spite of the fact that the bowl was discovered to be a fake, all kinds of places, including the middle of the Atlantic Ocean, Peru, Morocco, Nigeria and India, have been put forward as possible *sites* for the missing civilization. In the 1920s, the Scottish amateur archaeologist, Lewis Spence, maintained that at one time there had been a continent in the middle of the Atlantic. He argued that this had split into two island continents: Atlantis, not far to the west of Spain, and Antillia near the present West Indies. Then, according to Spence, the sub-continents sank in about 10,000 B.C., although parts of Antillia remained above the sea and formed the West Indian islands.

Right: This delicate fresco of a fisherman was found on Santorini. Much of the Minoans' art dealt with the sea.

Above: At one time, it was thought that Crete might have been Atlantis because it was believed its cities had been destroyed by a tidal wave caused by a volcanic eruption on Santorini.

Below: This pumice found among the remains of the Minoan harbour of Amnissos in Crete may be from a volcanic eruption in about 1400 B.C.

There is indeed a mid-Atlantic ridge running from Iceland in the north to the South Atlantic. The ridge is now a mile beneath the surface of the ocean and has great deeps to the east and west of it. In a few places, such as the Azores, Ascension Island and Tristan da Cunha, the ridge actually comes to the surface. Even if Spence's theory was correct, which is extremely unlikely, continents do not sink overnight as a result of a few earthquakes and tidal waves. A whole continent would take many millions of years to sink.

On the other hand, small areas of land have disappeared in similar circumstances. In fact, in 422 B.C., six years after the birth of Plato, the little Greek island of Atalante was swamped by a huge tidal wave caused by an earthquake. It is tempting to believe that Plato used this real, if minor, disaster as the basis for his famous story. Some historians are equally sure that Plato based his story on the collapse of the ancient Minoan civilization

of Crete 3500 years ago. Modern excavations have provided undeniable proof that Crete suffered a series of serious earthquakes, which are sometimes associated with tidal waves, during the Minoan period.

If Plato's Atlantis ever existed, it could be argued that its likeliest location would have been off south-western Spain. Some archaeologists believe that there was once a powerful city-state called Tartessos at the mouth of the Guadalquivir River. The Phoenicians, the famous traders from Tyre in Palestine, are supposed to have visited Tartessos and bought huge quantities of silver and other metals from its inhabitants. In about 631 B.C., a Greek merchant ship was carried as far as Tartessos by a storm and traded with its citizens. However, in about 500 B.C., all mention of the 'Silver City' ceased. Perhaps the port silted up and lost its trade. Perhaps it was destroyed by a tidal wave. As yet, no one knows for certain.

11

Search for the City

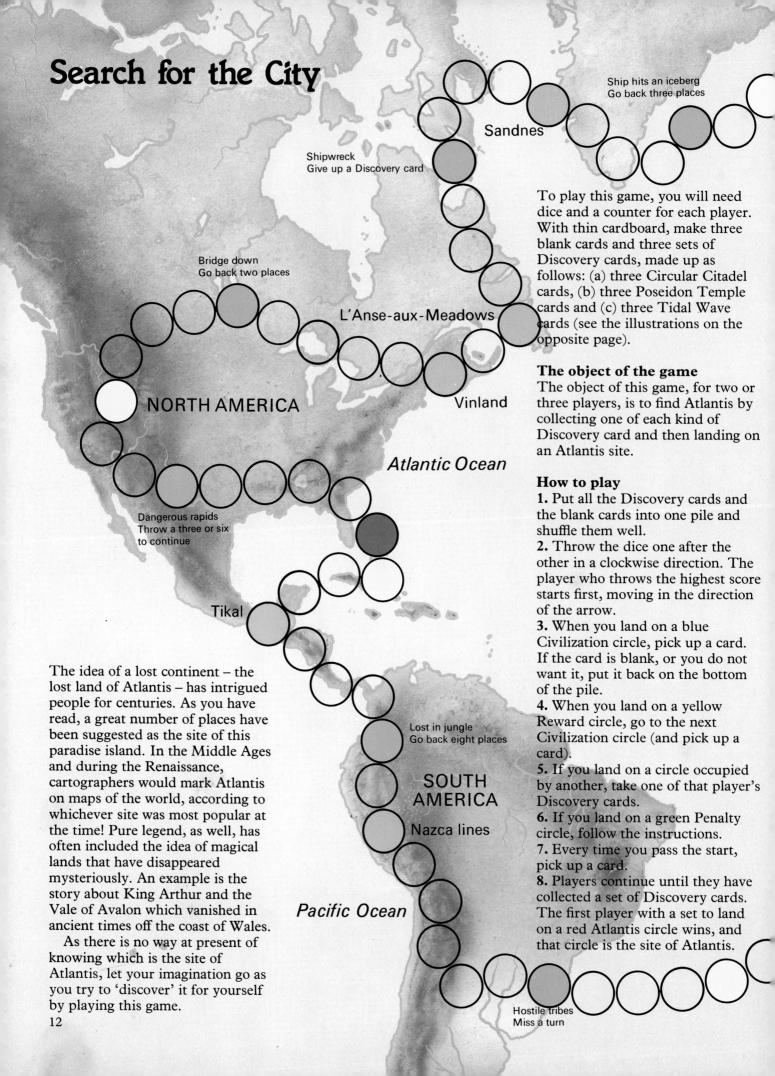

Ship hits an iceberg
Go back three places

Sandnes

Shipwreck
Give up a Discovery card

L'Anse-aux-Meadows

Bridge down
Go back two places

NORTH AMERICA

Vinland

Atlantic Ocean

Dangerous rapids
Throw a three or six
to continue

Tikal

Lost in jungle
Go back eight places

SOUTH
AMERICA

Nazca lines

Pacific Ocean

Hostile tribes
Miss a turn

To play this game, you will need dice and a counter for each player. With thin cardboard, make three blank cards and three sets of Discovery cards, made up as follows: (a) three Circular Citadel cards, (b) three Poseidon Temple cards and (c) three Tidal Wave cards (see the illustrations on the opposite page).

The object of the game
The object of this game, for two or three players, is to find Atlantis by collecting one of each kind of Discovery card and then landing on an Atlantis site.

How to play
1. Put all the Discovery cards and the blank cards into one pile and shuffle them well.
2. Throw the dice one after the other in a clockwise direction. The player who throws the highest score starts first, moving in the direction of the arrow.
3. When you land on a blue Civilization circle, pick up a card. If the card is blank, or you do not want it, put it back on the bottom of the pile.
4. When you land on a yellow Reward circle, go to the next Civilization circle (and pick up a card).
5. If you land on a circle occupied by another, take one of that player's Discovery cards.
6. If you land on a green Penalty circle, follow the instructions.
7. Every time you pass the start, pick up a card.
8. Players continue until they have collected a set of Discovery cards. The first player with a set to land on a red Atlantis circle wins, and that circle is the site of Atlantis.

The idea of a lost continent – the lost land of Atlantis – has intrigued people for centuries. As you have read, a great number of places have been suggested as the site of this paradise island. In the Middle Ages and during the Renaissance, cartographers would mark Atlantis on maps of the world, according to whichever site was most popular at the time! Pure legend, as well, has often included the idea of magical lands that have disappeared mysteriously. An example is the story about King Arthur and the Vale of Avalon which vanished in ancient times off the coast of Wales.

As there is no way at present of knowing which is the site of Atlantis, let your imagination go as you try to 'discover' it for yourself by playing this game.

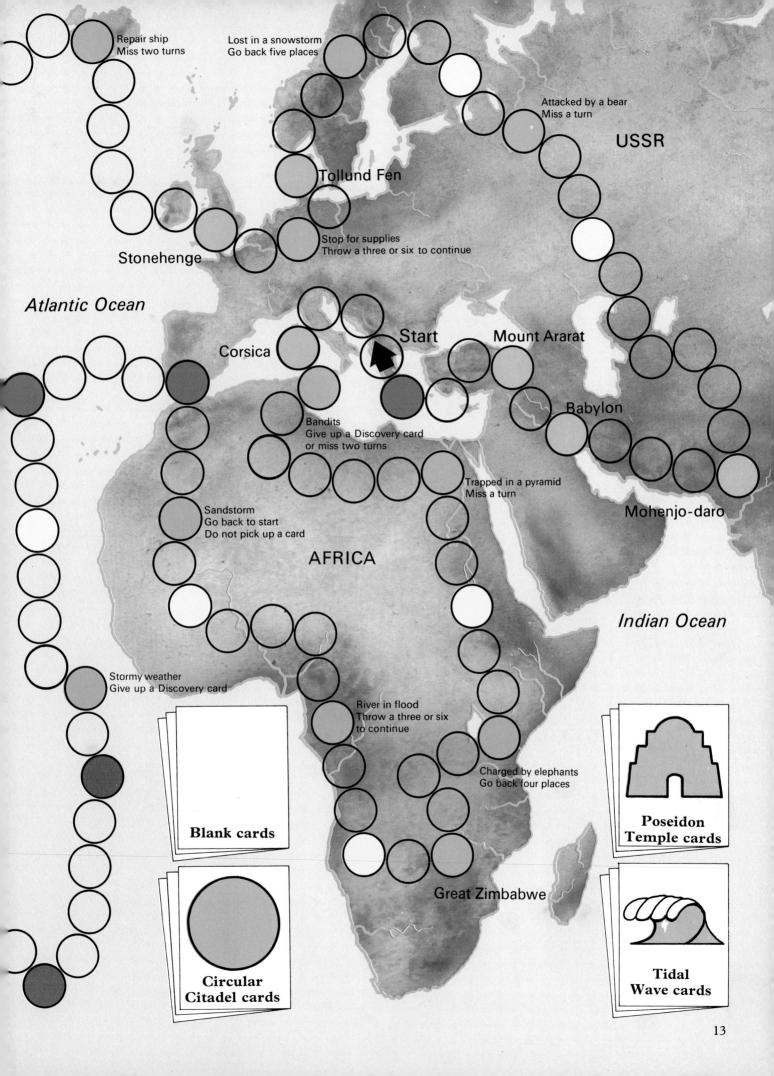

Repair ship
Miss two turns

Lost in a snowstorm
Go back five places

Attacked by a bear
Miss a turn

USSR

Tollund Fen

Stop for supplies
Throw a three or six to continue

Stonehenge

Atlantic Ocean

Corsica

Start

Mount Ararat

Babylon

Bandits
Give up a Discovery card
or miss two turns

Trapped in a pyramid
Miss a turn

Mohenjo-daro

Sandstorm
Go back to start
Do not pick up a card

AFRICA

Indian Ocean

Stormy weather
Give up a Discovery card

River in flood
Throw a three or six
to continue

Blank cards

Charged by elephants
Go back four places

**Poseidon
Temple cards**

**Circular
Citadel cards**

Great Zimbabwe

**Tidal
Wave cards**

13

Giants and Men

We watched them curiously. What were these strange creatures? In some ways, their appearance reminded me of the orang-utan. They present no problem. For all their undoubted strength, they are easy to trap. But these creatures were a very different matter. Their heads were massive and covered all over with coarse hair. My brother and I were filled with awe watching them tear at young bamboo shoots with huge jaws. And yet, were they so different from us? As we watched them, what we took to be an old male suddenly stood up and barked orders to the youngsters around him.

The animals were sitting at their ease in the long grass among some trees. The old male was continually watching for any danger and sniffing the breeze for the first scent of an enemy. The females fed their young placidly while the young males wrestled and rolled in the grass without a care in the world.

They looked harmless enough. But, when the old male rose to his feet, he was a gigantic size, nearly twice as tall as me – and I am considered tall. He and the other males in the group would be formidable enemies.

After resting during the hottest part of the day, the group set off again in the same determined but unhurried fashion with the old male in the lead. They moved with confidence as if they feared nothing. Determined to learn all we could about these strange beasts before returning to our own band, we followed them at a safe distance.

Having studied the gigantic creatures for some time, we were still undecided what to do about them. For many hours they had rambled through the open woodland, stopping now and again to crunch up some delectable fruit or shoot. I was beginning to relax when I realized that my brother was no longer beside me. He had moved closer to the edge of a clearing ahead and, unsuspecting,

was within touching distance of a female with two young who had become separated from the others. The old male was also nearby, partly hidden by some bushes. My brother called out and waved for me to follow him when, suddenly, before I could reach him, the male bore down on him swiftly and, with a petrifying roar, was upon him. We got away with our lives only because I stunned the male with my axe and we escaped, bleeding from our wounds, before the whole group could come upon us.

This awesome demonstration of strength decided me. These creatures were too dangerous to be allowed to roam in our territory. As long as they were alive, they might steal up on us and attack with the same dreadful ferocity that I had just witnessed. They must die.

The sun had gone down by the time we reached our camp. I then called a meeting of all the menfolk. Quickly and simply, I explained what had happened. Old Ay, the headman, agreed that no time should be lost. Arming ourselves with our best spears and sharpest axes, we made off into the night.

Just before dawn, we reached the giant apes' resting-place. They were still asleep. Swiftly, we marked the position of each animal and allotted a man to deal with it. I and two others chose to attack the old male.

Without further ado, we crept into their resting-place and were able to stab to death the majority of the beasts, while they were sleeping. Only the old male put up a real fight, killing one of us and smashing my spear arm before he himself was struck down.

It was over. We were safe for the time being and had an excellent supply of fresh meat which would last us many a week.

Right: A giant ape attacks prehistoric man. These apes probably roamed the open woodlands of China and India.

14

Dragons' Bones

Above: Fossilized teeth and jawbones of *Gigantopithecus* have been found in China and India.

Giants appear in fairy stories all over the world. Are they just something with which to frighten little children or is there some factual basis for the idea of a giant?

In 1935, the Dutch archaeologist, G. H. R. von Koenigswald, discovered a huge, man-like *fossil* tooth among the so-called 'dragon's bones' for sale in a Hong Kong chemist's shop. These bones are ground down by the Chinese and made into medicines. After careful examination, some scholars believed that the tooth was very old and belonged to the ancestor of Java Man and Peking Man who lived about 500,000 years ago. Von Koenigswald, however, insisted that the tooth must belong to some as yet unknown ape.

Since 1935, a large number of fossil remains of *Giganthropus* (Giant Man) or *Gigantopithecus* (Giant Ape) have been found which give a clearer picture of what this creature may have been like. By 1954, von Koenigswald had collected eight teeth, many of which could be dated to the geological period of time called the Middle Pleistocene, which was about 500,000 years ago. In the light of this new evidence, von Koenigswald changed his mind and decided that the teeth belonged

possibly to a giant ancestor of man.

In the meantime, Chinese archaeologists took over the investigation, headed by Professor W. C. Pei, who discovered not only large numbers of teeth, but a huge lower jaw-bone as well in the Chinese province of Kwangsi. By 1958, he had three lower jaw-bones and 1000 fossil teeth belonging to what he considered to be the giant ape. Even more exciting, a fourth enormous jaw-bone was found at Bilaspur, 200 miles north of New Delhi in the Siwalik Hills of India.

Man, the apes and *Old World* monkeys, which form part of the order of *primates* or higher mammals, have 32 teeth: 16 in each jaw. Each set contains four incisors, two canines, four premolars and six molars. In *Giganthropus* or *Gigantopithecus*, the incisors are small and peg-like. The canines, although large, are unlike those of any existing ape in that they have been worn flat by grinding food against the corresponding teeth in the other jaw. The molars are also very different from a modern ape's, in that these teeth are packed together towards the front of the

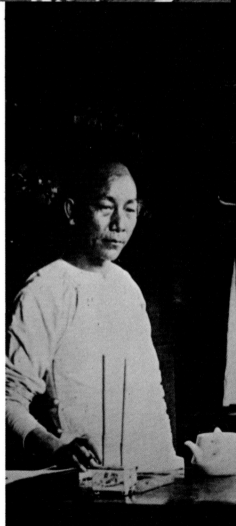

Left: The Chinese still believe in herbal medicines. Their pharmacists make tonics from plants and roots and from animal flesh and bones.

Right: These teeth belong to two species of giant ape which lived thousands of years ago. The larger tooth belonged to *Gigantopithecus* and the one above to *Dryopithecus*. Both are shown much enlarged.

Below: Pharmacies like this were to be found all over the Far East. It could well have been in such a shop that von Koenigswald first found the giant apes' fossil teeth.

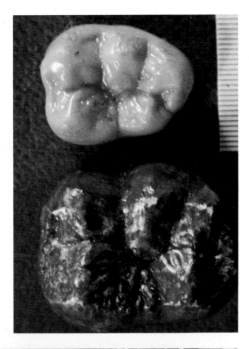

mouth. This means that the animal has had to chew hard materials.

If the rest of the animal's body was in proportion to its massive teeth and jaws, it must have weighed as much as 272 kilograms and been almost three metres tall when it stood upright on its hind legs. Such a huge animal would have had to eat and digest very efficiently large amounts of food to maintain its health and strength.

The kinds of fossil animals found with the giant help to a certain extent in the task of reconstructing its way of life. In the Kwangsi caves, the giant bones are found associated with those of orang-utan and various carnivorous animals. Unfortunately, all the bones look as if they had been gnawed by porcupines, so it may be that all the archaeologists found was a porcupine's food store!

It has been extremely difficult to date these remains, but it seems likely that the Chinese giants lived between 500,000 and a million years ago, while the Indian giants may have lived six million years ago or even earlier.

Now, most archaeologists think that the bones belong to the ancestor of a line of giant apes. The remains of a somewhat similar but earlier ape, called *Dryopithecus indicus*, have been found which may have been its ancestor. It, too, seems to have enjoyed the same kind of diet as man. After this, the ancestors of man and the great ape seem to have become more and more different.

But there is even more to this mystery. Some people believe that there may be descendants of *Giganthropus* or *Gigantopithecus* living in remote areas of the world today. There have been numerous reported sightings of a giant ape-like (or man-like!) creature from the Himalayas (the yeti or Abominable Snowman) to North America (the Bigfoot or the Sasquatch). Maybe there is some truth behind these sightings. What do you think?

17

Make a Giant Jaw-bone

Has there ever been a time in man's early history when there was a race of real giants? Throughout the Middle Ages, many people believed that giants were to be found in the then unknown lands of Africa and Asia. Even today people are fascinated by very tall peoples such as the Watussi of Zaire, some of whom are nearly three metres tall.

So strong was the belief in giants that archaeologists have searched hard and long for evidence of their existence. The remains of *Gigantopithecus* were hailed at first by Professor Weidenrich as those of a giant man. Even if he was correct, however, it is unlikely that we are the descendants of such a creature because examples of the bones of our ancestors have also been found in layers of rock from the same period of time.

Below: The fragment of one of the three *Gigantopithecus* jaws discovered so far. Its teeth closely resemble man's.

Right: In this illustration you can see the differences in size and shape between the jaw-bones of modern man (1), a modern gorilla (2) and *Gigantopithecus* (3).

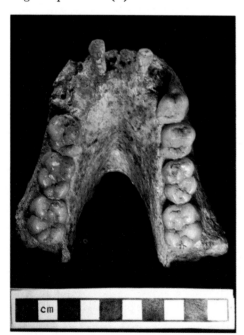

You will need: newspaper, foil, Mod-roc (buy this at a craft shop), modelling clay or plasticine, old bowl or foil dish, old pair of scissors, modelling tool.
1. Crumple the foil into the shape of the jaw-bone of *Gigantopithecus*, following the illustration below.

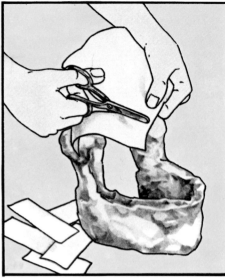

2. Cut a sheet of Mod-roc into *small* strips. (If you have no Mod-roc, you may use strips of old material, dipped into plaster of Paris mixed with water. You could also model the jaw-bone in clay or plasticine.)

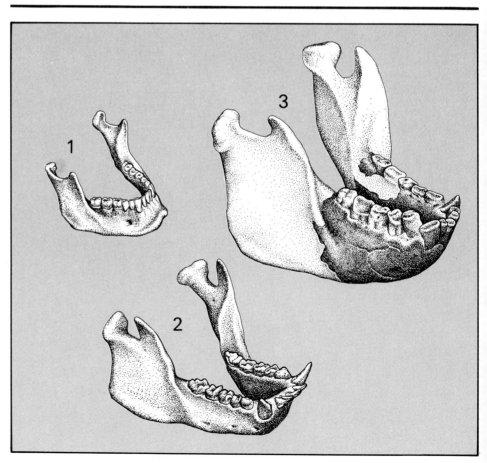

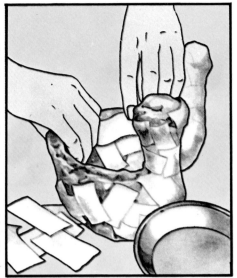

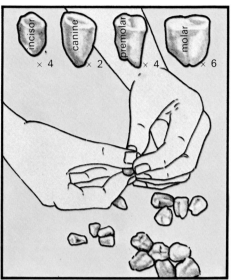

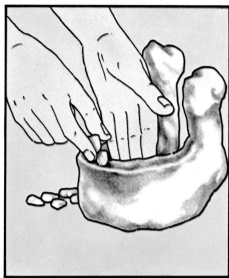

3. Dip one of the strips of Mod-roc into water and place on the foil, smoothing it into place. Continue doing this until the foil is covered, and the jaw-bone is the correct shape. Make sure you do not dip more than one piece of Mod-roc into water at a time, as it dries very quickly.

4. Put the jaw-bone to one side. Make 16 balls of clay (or plasticine) and model them into teeth. Model four incisors, two canines, four premolars and six molars (see the photograph below).

5. Position the teeth very carefully on the jaw-bone. Put the four incisors at the front and, either side of these, put one canine, followed by two premolars and three molars.

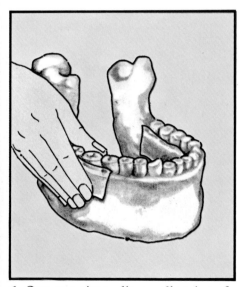

6. One at a time, dip small strips of Mod-roc into water and place them against the bottom edges of the teeth on both sides, to hold the teeth firmly in place. (*Remember that you must not* put any left-over plaster of Paris down the sink.)

7. The model of the jaw-bone.

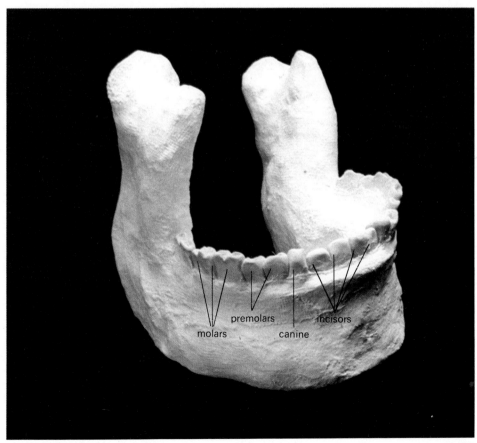

19

A Temple to the Sun

We, the people of the Plain, stood admiring the finished structure. There was an outer ring of thirty massive stones which had been hauled and rolled all the way from the Marlborough Downs where they had been quarried, to the site of our Temple at Stonehenge on Salisbury Plain. It was hot work. The great stones were lifted on to wooden sledges on top of rollers. Then, teams of sweating men tugged and pulled on the ropes attached to the stones until slowly but surely the ungainly blocks started to move forward. As the stones advanced, rollers were laid in front of them while the discarded ones were collected for re-use. In this way, slowly and with many a spill, the great *sarsen* stones were pushed and pulled all the way to the sacred place.

When the teams reached the site, encircled with a high bank and a deep ditch, they found that we were ready for them. Other men had already dug the pits for the stones to stand in. The sarsens were levered into the pits with wooden poles and gradually heaved upright by alternately lifting the stone and building up a supporting wall under it. Finally, the stones were hauled into the vertical position by great teams of labourers.

When the 30 stones were in position, the real work began. Smaller stones called *lintels* had to be placed on top of the pairs of sarsens. Log rafts were placed all round the sarsens and the lintels had to be levered up on to them. At last they lay alongside the tops of the uprights. Two knobs or tenons of stone had been left jutting out of the top of each sarsen while hollows or mortices had been scooped out of the lintels. Skilfully our men manoeuvred the lintels until at last the great stone circle was complete.

In the middle of the giant circle, a huge stone horseshoe was erected consisting of five giant arches or *trilithons*. Each trilithon consisted of a pair of huge uprights covered by a massive lintel.

Within the main circle and horseshoe of stones, another ring of 60 uprights and a horseshoe of 19 *bluestones* were set up. These stones also weighed a tremendous amount and had been brought all the way from the Prescelly Mountains in Wales. They had been hauled on wooden sledges down to the Severn Estuary, placed on rafts and sailed across the estuary and up the rivers Avon and Frome. From there, they were hauled overland to the River Wylye and up the Hampshire River Avon to within a short journey from Stonehenge.

At the very centre of the Temple, we placed a single mighty stone. This is where our priests will perform the sacred rites to Our Master the Sun. We also built a straight processional way which reaches to the banks of the River Avon. This way or Avenue is flanked on either side by great mounds and ditches, as the Holy Places may be approached only from the approved direction, and only the chosen may enter its sacred grounds. In the middle of the Avenue stands the sacred Sun Stone.

At the greatest moment of our year, Midsummer Day, the Sun will rise in all its glory and glint down the Avenue, casting a great shaft of light on to the Sun Stone and beyond into the very centre of Stonehenge itself. For a moment, our Lord and Master will show himself to his worshippers before gradually moving through the sky.

It is difficult to believe that our great work is actually finished. This place has been sacred to the gods since the world began. For as long as man shall live, these stones will stand as a testimony to our love and faith in the Sun.

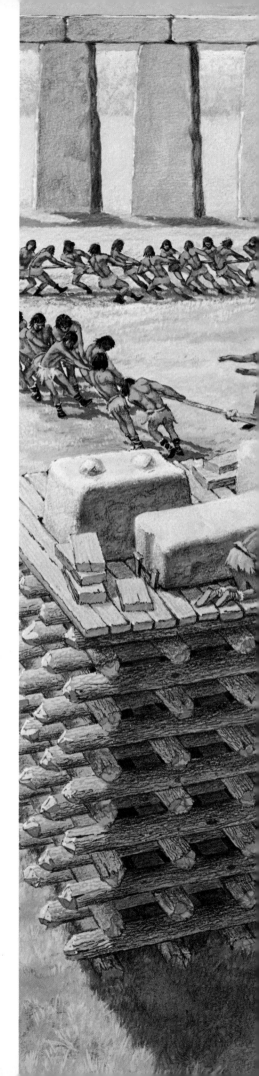

Right: Bronze-Age people built Stonehenge 3500 years ago. The circle was a religious centre, to which many pilgrims came.

20

Stonehenge

Above: Stonehenge, seen below at dawn, is located on Salisbury Plain in southern England.

Above: It was once thought, incorrectly, that the Celtic priests, called the Druids, built

Stonehenge. In this 18th-century engraving, the Druids celebrate a religious festival.

What is the fascination of Stonehenge? Why do thousands of visitors make their way to it by car and coach every year? Perhaps it is because an air of mystery still surrounds the huge Hanging Stones (a literal translation of the name 'Stonehenge'). Why did prehistoric men spend so long pushing and dragging these immense stones across Salisbury Plain? Why did they take such great care to shape the huge stones so that when you stare up at them they do not appear to bend or get smaller? No one knows for certain the answers to the many questions often asked about Stonehenge.

What was Stonehenge? Some experts believe that it was a temple, a kind of prehistoric cathedral. It seems likely that thousands of pilgrims from all over England made their way to the Hanging Stones. They probably crossed the River Avon and landed on the extreme edge of the Avenue. After walking for two miles between the great flanking mounds they arrived at what is now called the Heel Stone, a giant upright some four metres high. On reaching the holy circle, they would have entered between two enormous stone uprights. Only one of these monstrous posts remains and it has fallen to the ground. Nowadays, it is known as the 'Slaughter Stone' because early archaeologists thought it was an altar on which sacrificial victims were placed before being offered to the gods. However, there is no evidence that such sacrifices ever took place.

Even if Stonehenge was a temple, it may have been used for other purposes as well. Scientists believe that it is a *Stone-Age* computer which was used to predict eclipses of the sun and moon. If, as many think, prehistoric people worshipped the sun and moon, they must have been terrified when these were blotted out. During an eclipse of the sun, the moon is positioned between it and the Earth. This

means the sun is cut off from our view. On the other hand, a lunar eclipse is caused by the shadow which the Earth casts on the moon when the Earth is between the moon and the sun. Prehistoric people would have respected any group of experts who could predict when these frightening events were going to take place.

It may be that Stonehenge is a very elaborate kind of calendar. If you stand on the fallen Altar Stone in the centre of the stone circle, you can look right through the two sarsen pillars which form the

Above: Archaeologists used to think that the final version of Stonehenge was designed by a traveller to Britain from the Mediterranean world. The discovery of the carving of a dagger (the long shape in the centre) was seen as evidence.

Below: Compare this photograph of a reconstructed Mycenaean dagger with the carving of the dagger found at Stonehenge. You can see how similar they are in shape.

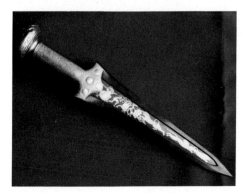

entrance to the Heel Stone beyond. On the first day of summer, the rising sun bathes the top of the Heel Stone in light. This, too, may have been very important for the early inhabitants of England, helping them to plan their year. Although these theories have been carefully checked out, there is not enough hard evidence to say whether they are right or wrong.

Who built Stonehenge? In the 17th and 18th centuries, many people thought that *Celtic* priests called *Druids* had ordered Stonehenge to be built. The Druids may have used Stonehenge but we now know that the Hanging Stones were erected long before there were any Druids in England. By testing the age of some charred bone found at Stonehenge, using the *radio-carbon dating* method, archaeologists have learnt that the bone was burnt about 3800 years ago. If Stonehenge was constructed at the same time, it must have been built about 1800 B.C.

But could primitive people have designed, organized and completed the construction of this marvel? In 1953, a carving of a short dagger was discovered on the inside face of one of the stone uprights. On careful examination, this carved dagger appeared to be somewhat like those used by the *Mycenaeans*, a civilized people who lived in ancient Greece. As a result of this discovery and certain supposed technical similarities with early Greek buildings, some archaeologists wonder whether Stonehenge was actually designed by a visiting Greek trader with an interest in architecture. On the other hand, there is no reason why these early inhabitants of England should not have planned and built Stonehenge on their own.

In spite of our greatly increased knowledge of Stonehenge, most of these really interesting questions remain matters of argument. The Hanging Stones still keep their unfathomable secrets.

Reconstruct the Past

Excavations and radio-carbon dating have shown that Stonehenge was developed over a period of about 1300 years. Building at the site on Salisbury Plain started in about 2800 B.C. and was completed in about 1550 B.C.

Today, Stonehenge is certainly impressive and awe-inspiring. The enormous size of the stones, placed as they are in such an exposed position, does much to make the onlooker feel quite insignificant. Each upright in the outer, 30-metre-wide Sarsen Circle weighs about 25 tonnes, with the sarsen lintels themselves weighing up to seven tonnes each. Each upright in the five giant trilithons weighs about 45 tonnes each.

Can you imagine what Stonehenge must have looked like before it became ruined, and as it must have appeared to the Stone-Age people of 3500 years ago when it was complete? Ask some friends to help reconstruct the scene.

You will need: modelling clay or plasticine, rolling pin, modelling tool, knife, stiff card 60 cm × 60 cm, string, two buttons, sticks, newspaper, paintbrush, green paint, gravel or sand.
1. Shape the clay (or plasticine) into a block. Use the string as shown to slice the clay.

Sarsen Circle
2. From the clay slices, cut out 30 shapes for the Sarsen Circle uprights (see the photograph of the model on the opposite page) with a knife or modelling tool, as shown above.

Below: This aerial view of Stonehenge shows the bank around it and the great avenue leading to the circle, along which pilgrims would have walked as they approached the sacred place.

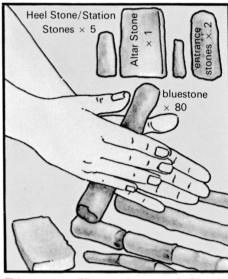

Heel Stone/Station Stones × 5
Altar Stone × 1
entrance stones × 2
bluestone × 80

Bluestone Horseshoe and Circle
6. Make these by rolling out a coil of clay (see the illustration above), and cutting it up into bluestones. Round off one end of each stone. You will need 20 stones for the horseshoe and 60 for the circle. Finish your model by making the Altar Stone and the other stones outside the circle.

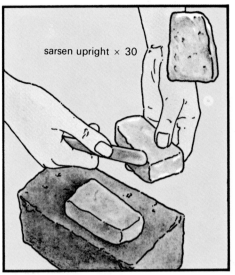

sarsen upright × 30

sarsen lintel × 30

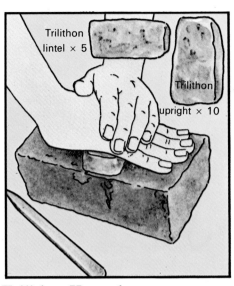

Trilithon lintel × 5

Trilithon upright × 10

3. Smooth and form each piece of clay into the shape of a sarsen upright. To give the stones a natural, uneven finish, press them firmly against the rough surface of a brick.

4. Roll out a slice of clay, using two sticks as guides. Score it into strips and then smaller rectangular blocks (30 in all) with a modelling tool, to make the Sarsen Circle lintels, then cut out. Smooth all the edges.

Trilithon Horseshoe
5. Make the trilithon uprights and lintels in the same way as you made the sarsen uprights and lintels (follow steps 2–4), but make them slightly larger. You will need ten uprights and five lintels.

7. Use card for the base and paint it green. When dry, sprinkle fine gravel (or sand) in the centre of the card and position your model as shown on the right, pushing the uprights firmly into the gravel.

8. It is interesting to compare the model with the aerial photograph of Stonehenge on the left.

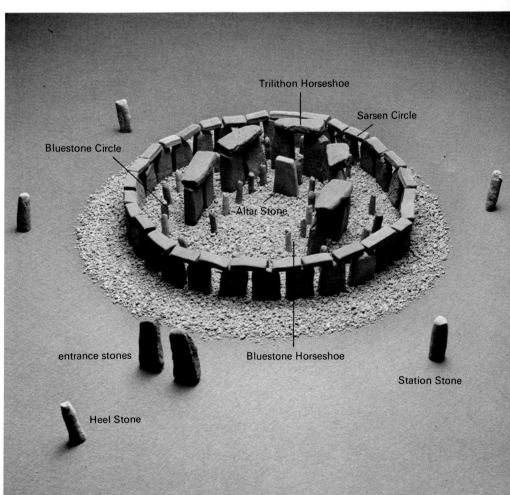

Trilithon Horseshoe

Sarsen Circle

Bluestone Circle

Altar Stone

entrance stones

Bluestone Horseshoe

Station Stone

Heel Stone

The Attack

'The *barbarians* are coming! The barbarians are coming!' So rang the cry among the panic-stricken people of Mohenjo-daro in the Indus River Valley of Pakistan more than three and a half centuries ago. News had spread through the empire that invaders from the north were coming whose warriors were tall and strong.

Mohenjo-daro was one of the capitals of the once mighty empire that had included the whole of the Indus Valley. The city was dominated by a citadel whose towers and walls were now decayed and unkempt. Inside the citadel, however, you could still glimpse the glory of the once all-powerful High Priests. Two beautiful pillared halls dominated the area. In the first hall, ordinary people were able to approach the ruler at certain times of the day to deliver petitions. In the second, even more gorgeous chamber, the ruler received his nobles and generals.

Beyond the halls and the High Priests' living quarters lay the Sacred Bath. The faithful came here to bathe in the holy waters before making their offerings to the most high and powerful gods. Sadly, everything about the once gorgeous palace complex created an impression of neglect and faded splendour. From a distance the city looked as impressive as ever. On closer inspection, however, you could see that many of the magnificent old houses had been carelessly repaired with old, rotten bricks. Worse still, in the working people's quarters, the clean cottages of earlier periods had been replaced by shoddily built slums.

Now the streets were empty, even though the enemy was at the gates. The once brave and courageous people waited for the barbarians to arrive. They could have seized their valuables and tried to escape, but what was the use? There was no escape. Towards morning, trumpets were blown on the citadel. The moment had come.

In the bloody light of the rising sun, columns of chariots could be seen approaching the city with regiments of foot-soldiers marching on each side of them. On reaching the outskirts of the city, the barbarians smashed their way through the thin line of defending soldiers and poured into the straight streets. Mercilessly, they set about killing the inhabitants, not even sparing the crying women and children.

The fighting now shifted to the citadel. Here, the few remaining defenders made their last stand, encouraged by their screaming priests. However, their courage was gone. After a brief struggle, the barbarians forced their way through the main gateway. The guards tried to surrender but were butchered where they stood. The raiders swept through the pillared halls helping themselves to the treasures and killing the few remaining priests they found cowering in the cells. Soon, the citadel was as desolate as the rest of the town.

By the time the slaughter was over, the streets and houses were filled with the dead. The invaders left them where they lay. Once the barbarians had stolen all that attracted them, they moved on. The few people who had survived emerged from their hiding places and fled to the jungle-clad hills.

Year after year and generation after generation, the city remained desolate and empty. Weeds grew up everywhere. Young trees pushed up through the paving and under walls until they collapsed. Nature started to close in on the crumbling ruins. The mud-brick buildings turned to powder. Soon, all that remained of the once mighty empire were a few mounds of earth covered by rich vegetation.

Right: Aryan invaders attack the town of Mohenjo-daro in the Indus Valley and kill its inhabitants, including a priest. Soon, the town will be desolate.

The Indus Civilization

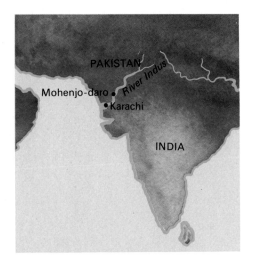

Above: The town of Mohenjo-daro was built on the west bank of the River Indus in Pakistan.

Everything about the Indus Valley civilization is mysterious. Who created it? Normally, when civilizations develop, archaeologists can find evidence of a gradual improvement in agriculture, cattle-breeding and metal-working in the area. Small villages become large villages and eventually cities. As far as can be discovered, the Indus civilization originated suddenly in about 2500 B.C. All kinds of theories have been put forward to explain this mystery. Some people think that the Indus civilization was really Plato's lost land of Atlantis. Others argue that the civilization must have been started by skilled people who had emigrated from ancient Sumeria or Egypt. Unfortunately, although the latter theory seems very reasonable, the Indus Valley civilization seems to have been very different from that of either of the other two.

Superb towns such as Mohenjo-daro were built with great citadels, as well as huge baths which may have been used for religious purposes. The towns were divided up into blocks by straight roads which crossed each other at right angles. Every house and every street was connected to one of the most advanced drainage systems developed in the ancient world.

The people seem to have been strictly controlled for, as you have just read, the towns were carefully planned. The wheat and barley grown by the peasants seems to have been stored in state granaries; fine buildings of this kind have been found in many of the Indus Valley cities. And yet no royal tombs have been found, so who were the rulers? The simplest explanation may be that the archaeologists have not yet come across royal tombs, because there is still a great deal of work to be done on most of the sites. Or could it be that the Indus people were ruled by High Priests or groups of nobles who did not receive special burials?

How could these ancient people afford to build their magnificent cities? In order to do so, the richer classes must have had plenty of leisure time and the means of controlling large numbers of labourers. It seems they had the leisure time as they were very successful farmers. From fragments of grain and seeds found on the Indus Valley sites, we know that crops grown included large quantities of wheat, barley, field-peas and melons. Oil was obtained from sesame and mustard seeds. They had domesticated dogs, cats,

Left: Streets in Mohenjo-daro were straight and crossed each other at right angles.

humped cattle, short-horned cattle and buffaloes as well as pigs, camels, horses, asses and possibly elephants. Certainly, the Indus people were rich enough to import luxuries such as turquoise.

Equally astonishing is this great empire's decline. Once again all kinds of theories have been suggested to explain the facts. Some archaeologists believe that the sea coast was rising and that this caused severe flooding. However, other experts suggest that the Indus people brought about important and ultimately disastrous climatic changes in the area by cutting down vast areas of forest with which to bake bricks. This is thought to have led to a reduction in frequency of the rainfall. When the rains did come they were probably torrential, causing soil erosion and eventually a decline in the fertility of the soil. Another theory is that the Indus peoples kept such vast herds of cattle that they overgrazed the plains. Certainly there is abundant archaeological evidence to prove that the Indus cities deteriorated slowly over a long period of time.

It seems likely that the declining civilization was brought to an abrupt end by invaders. There are many examples of sudden and violent death among the last inhabitants of the important town of Mohenjo-daro. The skeletons of murdered people have been found sprawled among the ruins. Who were the invaders? The most likely candidates are the Aryans who settled down and took over the Indus valley. In one of their holy books, the *Rigveda*, there are descriptions of chariot-driving warriors led by the god Indra, the 'Fort-Destroyer', conquering great lands. Perhaps these accounts refer to the destruction of the Indus peoples.

Before any final decision can be made, a great deal more work will have to be done on the ancient Indus ruins.

Above: The Great Bath at Mohenjo-daro may have been used for religious purposes.

Right: An impression made by a cylinder seal shows a bull. Seals like this one, found at Mohenjo-daro, were used by the Indus peoples to mark property. The script on the seal has not yet been translated.

Below: Indus farmers hauled grain to the cities in ox-drawn carts. Similar carts are still used today.

Make an Indus Ox-cart

The two-wheeled ox-cart that we show you how to make on these pages is based upon models or toys found at Mohenjo-daro in Pakistan. The Indus people also used larger, four-wheeled wagons. Both carts and wagons would have been used to bring grain from all over the Indus valley to the enormous city granaries such as the one whose remains have been excavated at Mohenjo-daro. Forty-five centuries later, the people of Pakistan and India are still using very similar carts and wagons.

You will need: balsa-wood $7\frac{1}{2}$ cm × $9\frac{1}{2}$ cm × 4 mm (floor), 6 cm × 12 cm × 3 mm (wheels), 42 cm × 5 mm × 5 mm (pole and yoke), 30 cm × 1 cm × 1 cm (supports); dowelling $9\frac{1}{2}$ cm × 3 mm diameter (axle); fine sandpaper, clear glue, fretsaw (or craft knife), metal ruler, pencil, compass, knitting needle, cocktail sticks, pipe-cleaner, pins, scissors.

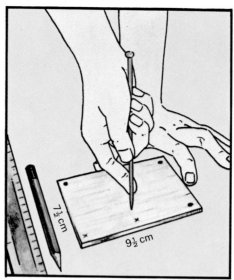

1. Measure a piece of balsa-wood for the floor of the cart and cut with a fretsaw. With a pencil, mark the positions of the six guard-poles and, with a fine steel knitting needle, make six holes very carefully so as not to split the wood.

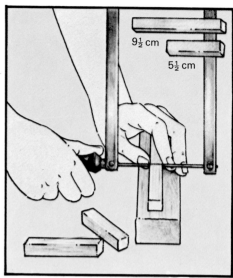

2. Measure two pieces of wood $9\frac{1}{2}$ cm × 1 cm × 1 cm and two more $5\frac{1}{2}$ cm × 1 cm × 1 cm for the supports, and cut to length. If necessary, smooth down the ends with sandpaper.

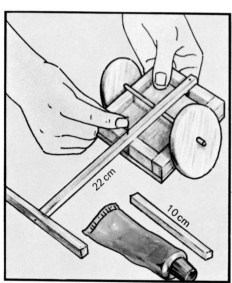

6. Measure one length of balsa-wood 22 cm long for the cart-pole, and two other pieces each 10 cm long for the yoke, and cut them. Glue and pin the lower part of the yoke to the cart-pole, then fasten the cart-pole to the cart in the same way.

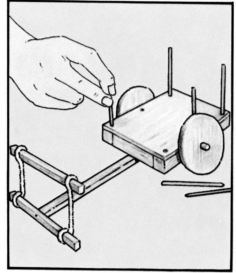

7. Attach the upper part of the yoke to the lower part of the yoke with two short lengths of pipe-cleaner, as shown. Put the guard-poles in place (smooth off the sharp ends of the cocktail sticks with sandpaper).

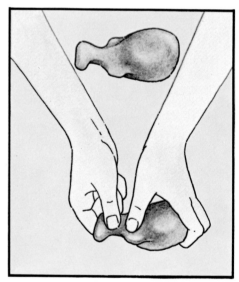

The oxen

You will need: modelling clay or plasticine.

8. Model the body from a ball of clay. Model the head from a smaller ball of clay and mould on to the body. Repeat for the second ox.

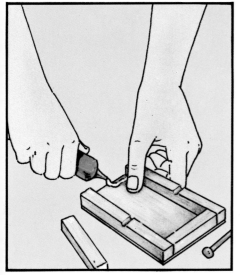

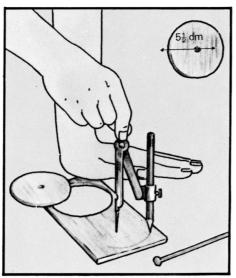

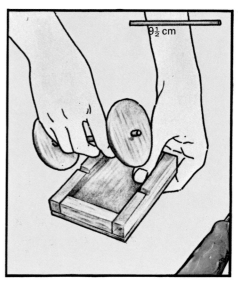

3. Take the two longer pieces of wood that will hold the axle. With a knitting needle, make a shallow groove across the centre of each piece, deep enough to take the dowelling. Glue all four supports in place.

4. For the wheels, draw two circles 5½ cm in diameter on to the balsawood (these can also be made in card). Cut with a fretsaw. Make a hole in the centre of each wheel (big enough to take the dowelling) with a knitting needle.

5. Measure a piece of dowelling 9½ cm long for the axle and cut. Attach the wheels and glue the dowelling in place.

9. Make the legs for each ox from thin coils of clay (do not stand the oxen up until the clay is firm). Add the ears and horns.

10. After you have put the oxen in place, you can add a touch of realism by loading the cart.

The Prophecy

Nebuchadnezzar, the great king of Babylon in Mesopotamia, sat at ease in his luxurious palace gardens. Breathing in air perfumed by a thousand rare plants and listening to the musical tinkling of the streams and waterfalls, the mighty king dozed.

The gardens had been built at great cost for Amyitis, the daughter of the powerful king of the Medes, who had reluctantly become his bride many years before. The homesick girl had pined for the green hills and cool breeze of her native home in Media during her first months in the heat of an airless, sun-scorched Babylon. Normally, Nebuchadnezzar ignored the whinings and complaints of his wives, but he could not afford to do this in the case of Amyitis. She was a Mede and the great king saw that it would be wise not to quarrel with these people and their neighbours, the Persians.

For the sake of his god Marduk and his empire, he had swallowed his pride and made every effort to reconcile his unhappy bride to her new way of life. A series of *terraces* had been built upon vaulted arches beside the palace, then filled with rich earth and planted with trees and flowers of all kinds. All this the proud Nebuchadnezzar had done to maintain his friendship with the Medes and the Persians.

He began his reign in 605 B.C. and during his 42 years of power he had certainly never shown any signs of weakness. He had destroyed the cruel Assyrians and defeated the Egyptians. He had terrified the Jews into submission and, when they dared to revolt, he had destroyed Jerusalem and had brought most of its inhabitants as slaves to Babylon. And yet, in spite of all these victories, the great king still felt uneasy. Was his empire really safe? Perhaps the wretched Jews were the source of all his fears. Were they not always mumbling that their god would punish the Babylonians for

destroying his precious temple and taking away his chosen people from the promised land?

Awakening suddenly from his doze, all these worrying thoughts began to go through his mind. Nebuchadnezzar stared about him angrily and a strong feeling of injustice came over him. Had he not done everything that the mighty Marduk could desire? He had forced millions of people to bow down and worship him. He had rebuilt Marduk's capital, Babylon, and made it a place of unequalled splendour and beauty.

The holy city was surrounded by walls of immense size and strength. Why, they were so wide that chariots could be driven on top of them without danger or difficulty! The giant gateways were covered with bright tiles and guarded by fierce stone monsters as well as trained soldiers. From the main gate ran the glorious Processional Way down which Nebuchadnezzar had dragged many thousands of weary prisoners of war to present them to the all-powerful Marduk.

As Nebuchadnezzar lay upon his golden bed that night, he continued to worry about the future of Babylon. The Medes and Persians, those wretched mountain-dwellers, would destroy his people unless they took heed of his warnings. When Nebuchadnezzar awoke, he summoned his family, his ministers and his generals and told them of his fears. Glancing from face to face, he saw nothing but disbelief and contempt beneath their studied expressions of respect. Suddenly, he felt old and tired. With a feeble gesture, he dismissed them.

Within two days, the king was dead and his words were forgotten. But, in 539 B.C., Cyrus the Persian king and his army took mighty Babylon without striking a blow. The prophecy had been fulfilled.

Right: King Nebuchadnezzar rests in the Hanging Gardens of Babylon, near the Ishtar Gate.

The Hanging Gardens of Babylon

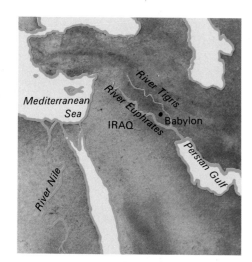

Above: Babylon was built on the east bank of the Euphrates River in Mesopotamia.

According to the writers of the ancient world, the Hanging Gardens of Babylon were one of the seven wonders of the world. People came from far and near to see them suspended 'between Heaven and Earth'. For centuries there was no physical evidence to show that they had ever existed. Then, between 1899 and 1917, a German archaeologist, Robert Koldewey, slowly uncovered the ancient city of Babylon, situated in what is now Iraq. First of all, he exposed the city walls, which were covered in debris to a depth of between nine and 24 metres. There were in fact three sets of walls, one inside the other. Running along the base of the inside wall, there was a deep *fosse* or moat which could be flooded in times of danger.

Much of the rebuilding and embellishing of Babylon was done about 2500 years ago. The walls were pierced by eight wide gateways from which huge copper-covered cedarwood doors had hung. The most famous is the Ishtar Gate, decorated with reliefs of more than 150 lions, bulls and dragons. In their heyday, these fortifications must have been a blaze of colours, as their blue and yellow enamelled tiles glinted in the bright sunlight.

An impressive Processional Way led through the Ishtar Gate and passed between palaces, temples

Left: Visitors to ancient Babylon entered the city through the Ishtar Gate. Its walls were covered by 13 rows of brilliantly coloured dragons and bulls, arranged in such a way that they appeared to march towards the visitors. The dragon was sacred to the most important god, Marduk, and his son Nabu. Ishtar was the goddess of Love and War.

Below: Carvings or reliefs of bulls, such as this one from the Ishtar Gate, represented Adad, god of rain and storms.

and private houses on its way to the religious centre of the mighty city.

On one side stood the Temple of Marduk, which had once contained the god's golden shrine. In ancient times, kings had gone there to seek Marduk's blessing or to give thanks for their victories. The temple was the centre of a great complex of buildings including living quarters for priests and civil servants as well as gardens, stables and kennels for the god's sacred dogs.

Opposite the Temple of Marduk stood a towering *ziggurat*, the so-called Tower of Babel. This seven-tiered structure reached a height of 90 metres. Each storey or tier was painted a different colour: white,

black, blue, yellow, silver and gold (the seventh colour is not known). Although every Babylonian city had its ziggurat, no other could compare with Babylon's. Fifty-eight million bricks had been used in its construction and thousands of pilgrims made their way to it each year. It stood in the middle of a huge enclosure containing the apartments and offices of many priests and officials. In addition, it is believed that stores of gold, silver and precious stones as well as a collection of chariots, couches and thrones were kept there.

Between the Ishtar Gate and the Tower of Babel lay the Palace of King Nebuchadnezzar. This was

constructed around five great courtyards. The palace contained not only the royal apartments but government offices as well as guardrooms for the royal bodyguard. To the south of the palace lay a huge throne room. This magnificent chamber, measuring 52 by 17 metres, was painted blue and decorated with columns topped by double capitals which were enamelled in gold, black, white, yellow and red. The doorways were adorned with brightly coloured friezes of lions.

But where in all this magnificence were the Hanging Gardens? Near the Ishtar Gate, Koldewey discovered a curious arched structure. Amongst its ruins, there were the shafts of a triple well. Further study revealed that the brick arches had been reinforced with stone, which was most unusual in Babylonian buildings. After carefully re-reading all the ancient accounts of the gardens, Koldewey finally announced that he had discovered what was probably the remains of the Hanging Gardens. The reinforced arches, he argued, had supported an extensive terraced garden. Water from the triple well to irrigate the gardens had been raised to the terraces by some machine which had long since crumbled away. The terraces would have been made waterproof by lining them with baked brick, bitumen and lead. The Hanging Gardens were not magical structures suspended between Heaven and Earth but elaborate roof gardens.

But no archaeological evidence has come to light as yet to prove that it was actually King Nebuchadnezzar who had the gardens built. Other legends say the gardens were made by Semiramis, a queen of ancient Assyria. It is not even known for certain that what Koldewey excavated were the fabled gardens. The legend still holds its magic and mystery.

Above: These are the excavated remains of what Robert Koldewey thought must have been the Hanging Gardens of Babylon. It is still not certain who erected the gardens. It may have been King Nebuchadnezzar, but an ancient clay tablet has been found which tells of another Babylonian king called Marduk-apal-iddin. He was interested in plants, especially herbs, which he planted in the 'Great Garden'.

A Miniature Garden

In the north-eastern corner of the palace of King Nebuchadnezzar in Babylon, Robert Koldewey discovered some puzzling ruins. Careful study revealed a large structure made up of two rows of seven vaulted chambers. Curiously, the walls of the inner rooms were thicker and stronger than those of the outer ones. Koldewey deduced that the middle arches had been built to bear heavier weights than the outer ones, and decided that such a structure would have supported roof gardens similar to those described by ancient writers as the Hanging Gardens of Babylon.

You will need: stiff card (or old boxes), rubber-based glue, poster paints, paintbrush, metal ruler, knitting needle, pencil, scissors, craft knife, sticky tape, paper-clips, gravel, dried flowers, plants.

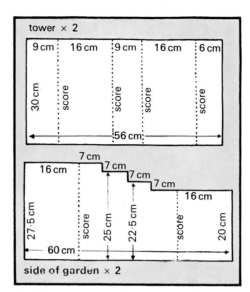

1. Measure two pieces of card 56 cm × 30 cm for the two towers and two pieces of card 60 cm × 27·5 cm for the sides of the garden. Cut out. Draw and cut the shapes for the four terraces on each side of the garden, as shown. Paint or cover with paper.

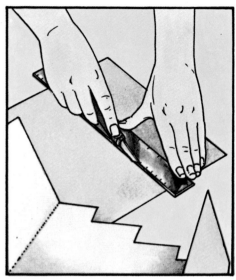

2. Score the pieces of card where indicated in step 1. To score, cut the surface of the card lightly with a knife against the edge of a metal ruler. Fold the card carefully along the scored line, which may be strengthened with sticky tape.

6. Put some plants into the smallest pots you can find. Mark where the pots will go on the floors and cut out the holes. Make sure the pots fit firmly into the holes. With a knitting needle, make tiny holes to take dried flowers.

7. Glue the four terraces together and then glue these into the centre section of the garden. Glue the tower floors into place, as well. If necessary, use sticky tape to make the building more secure.

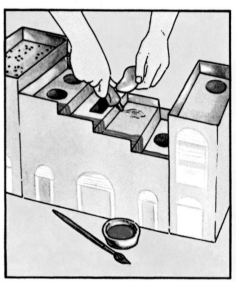

8. Paint the stream and waterfalls with poster paints or stick on coloured paper. You can use small pieces of broken mirror or scraps of foil for ponds.

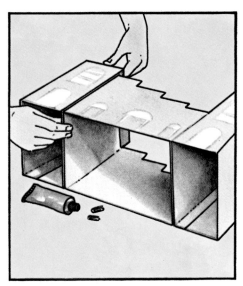

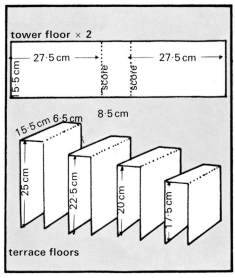

3. Paint the arches (or stick on paper shapes) on the front of the towers and terraces. Glue the towers then the two sides of the terraces together. Secure with paper-clips until dry.

4. Glue the three sections of the Hanging Gardens together and hold these firm with paper-clips until the glue is dry.

5. Measure two pieces of card 63·5 cm × 15·5 cm for the floors of the towers. Cut and score where indicated. Make the floors of the terraces from four pieces of card: 56·5 cm, 51·5 cm, 46·5 cm, 41·5 cm long (each 15·5 cm wide). Cut and score where indicated.

9. Put the plants in place. If you find that extra support is needed, use cardboard cylinders as a support (such as the ones found inside rolls of kitchen foil). Sprinkle fine gravel around the plants.

10. Do not forget to water the plants in your garden regularly.

The Great Rebellion

'Death to the priests! Death to the idle parasites!' bellowed the mob of angry Mayan peasants, brandishing stone knives, spears and digging sticks. For countless years they had toiled making clearings in the jungle to grow maize, and always bowed their heads at the mention of the sacred name. Normally, they referred to maize as 'Your Grace'. For years, they had accepted that the priests and nobles were their superiors and that it was their duty to raise crops and pay taxes so that their betters could build and maintain the Houses of the Gods. But, in return, they expected the priests to keep the gods happy and to let them know when to sow their crops. During the last few years, the priests had become careless. More and more frequently they had given the peasants bad advice and the crops had become poorer year by year. As a result, the people had starved and died of all kinds of mysterious fevers.

When they dared to complain, the priests ordered them back to the fields. Month after month they slaved, cutting down the jungle with stone axes and burning it. In the rich ashes they planted their maize but, as time passed, the gods only responded by punishing them with storms and disease. The time had come for the people to overthrow their idle masters.

Mobs of angry peasants converged on Tikal, the ancient capital in the Petén. Long before they reached the city walls, they could see the towering pyramids with the sacred temples on top. For centuries they had been proud that they had built more temple-pyramids than any other city-state in the Mayan lands. Now, they wanted proof that the gods existed. There had been terrible rumours that there were no gods and that the wicked priests and nobles had been growing fat by eating the peasants' hard-won crops.

Soon, the great columns of angry workers burst through the gates,

cutting down the few temple guards who dared to bar their way. The peasants made their way to the great square before the temple-pyramids. There they found the High Priests, some nobles and warriors waiting for them. For a moment, the peasants hung back, filled with the old awe and fear. Then, with a roar of rage, they surged forward, engulfing their enemies.

In the sacred places, the people laid about them, breaking the upright stones, the holy *stelae*, in two. Mobs ran howling up the steps of the pyramids and entered the dark, gloomy temples which had been closed to them before. Awe-struck, they looked about them. But where were the gods? No one struck them down with a bolt of lightning! With a laugh, they set about looting whatever took their fancy. In the great libraries, the labourers stared in confusion at the holy folding books. What did all these weird *glyphs* mean? But what did it matter, it was all lies. How well the books burnt, throwing weird dancing shadows on the stone walls.

By the next morning, it was all over. The holy places had been pillaged. Once more the rain was pouring down. Once more their crops would spoil. The gods were still angry. What could they do now? Nothing but start all over again. Already, groups of labourers were trying to restore the broken and defaced stelae.

Unfortunately, it was difficult to tell which way up they were supposed to go as nobody could read the glyphs. Still, perhaps it would not be long before new priests appeared and life returned to normal. What was certain, however, was that the old order would never be the same again.

Right: Angry Mayan peasants loot the temples and kill the nobles and warriors in the city of Tikal.

The Maya

Above: The religious centre of Tikal lies in the Petén district of Guatemala.

Above: It is still not certain whether Tikal was a city or just a religious centre. On some Mayan sites there is evidence that nobles lived in them. Many ordinary people's houses may have vanished, being made of perishable materials.

Right: This upright stone, found at Tikal, is called a stela. Some stelae had religious importance and many had inscriptions carved on them, which scholars are still deciphering.

In the dense tropical jungles of northern Guatemala in Central America, explorers such as the Spanish priest, Bishop de Landa, in the 16th century, had discovered a number of mysterious deserted cities. But it was not until after the travels of Alfred Maudslay in 1881–2 that the site of Tikal in the Petén region of Guatemala became known in Europe. This city, probably one of the oldest and most important of the Mayan cities, was found surrounded by tropical forest swarming with a rich variety of birds and animals.

Twelve hundred years ago, the city was dominated by a half-hectare plaza or square surrounded by great temple-pyramids and palaces. More stone pyramids were to be found at intervals in all directions. Narrow streets led from building to building, and raised paved causeways linked all the hills on which Tikal was built.

The temple-pyramids were the most impressive buildings. Some were as high as a modern 20-storey skyscraper. Their sides rose steeply and great flights of steps led to the top. The temples at the top were small, dark and oppressive, with huge stone comb-like decorations perched on their roofs. Rows of stelae or carved upright stones

surrounded the pyramids. Sacrificial victims had their heads cut off and were then thrown down the steps of the temple-pyramids. There were also drum-shaped altars on which it is believed that purification rituals were carried out.

Almost every aspect of the life of the ancient Maya seems to have been connected with their religion. Even their sports and games appear to have served religious purposes. Of particular importance seems to have been a ball game which combined some of the features of basketball and rugby. It was played with a rubber ball in great stone courts with rings instead of baskets fixed into the walls.

Carvings found on many sites show that the priests spent much time working out calendars. They had no less than three of these which went back thousands of years. We still have a lot to learn about this mysterious obsession, as Mayan writing is difficult to decipher and most of their *codices* or folding books have been destroyed.

The Maya were basically a farming people. They cleared the forest with stone axes, burnt the trees and planted maize and root crops such as yams in the rich ashes. These clearings were called *milpas*. The maize and root crops were eked out with beans, tomatoes and peppers. During good years, they grew enough food to allow them to spend much of their time building their religious centres.

When Tikal was re-discovered in the 19th century, it had been deserted for hundreds of years. Archaeologists have established that the Maya abandoned it some time between A.D. 800 and 1000. Why? Many explanations have been put forward such as earthquakes, changes in climate, disease, invasion, civil war and over-cultivation of the land. However, there is no geological evidence of earthquakes or climatic changes. Nor do there appear to have been any epidemic diseases in Central America sufficiently lethal to wipe out whole populations. There is no evidence of invasion at Tikal.

On the other hand, it is possible that the Maya exhausted the soil with their crude *slash-and-burn agriculture* and that, because of this, they suffered from diseases caused by eating crops with very little nutrition in them. This, together with many other problems, made the Mayan peasants rebel and destroy their priests and nobles. As a result, their rich civilization declined and many people deserted their homes and moved to cities further to the north-east. Certainly, archaeologists have found large numbers of broken stelae at Tikal and other Mayan centres. Some had been thrown on to rubbish dumps while others had been stuck back into the ground upside-down, as if someone had been trying to restore the holy places but could not read the strange signs carved on the upright stones.

The mystery of the collapse of Tikal and the other Mayan cities remains unsolved. What do you think happened?

Below: Here is a copy of part of the Dresden codex, one of the three Mayan folding books that have survived. This chapter is concerned with the planet Venus.

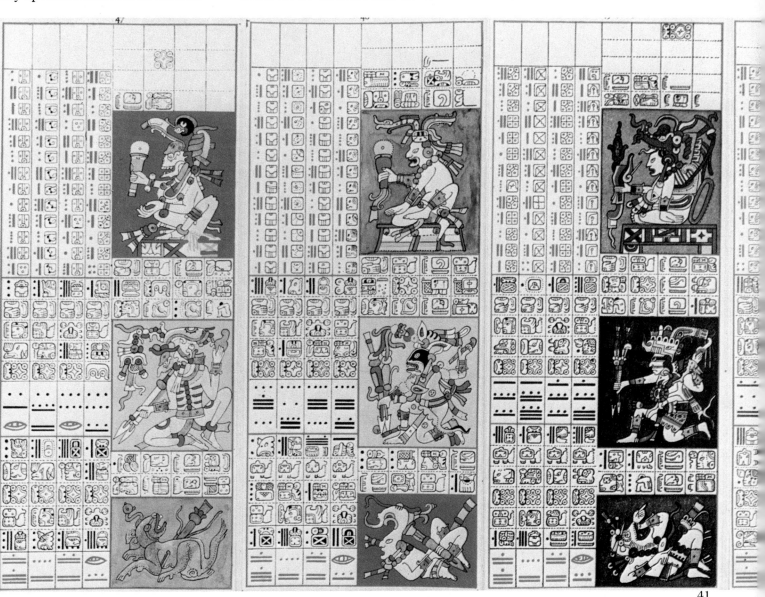

Paint a Mayan Folding Book

Mayan codices or books were 'written' on long strips of bark from a wild fig tree, pounded into long, thin sheets which were then stuck back to back. Deerskin was also used. Both sides of the page were covered with a coating of white lime, which strengthened the sheets as well as acting as a base for painting. Glyphs (picture-letters) were painted on the sheets.

A whole series of pages was joined to form a complete folding book. The pages read from top to bottom and from left to right.

Out of the hundreds of Mayan codices that must have been written, unfortunately only three have survived. In 1562, the Spanish priest Bishop Diego de Landa had all the books burnt because he believed they 'contained ... superstition and lies of the devil'.

Below: This part of the Dresden codex (folding book) describes Mayan New Year ceremonies.

You will need: stiff card (black), cartridge paper, sticky tape, poster paints, paintbrush, pencil, tracing paper, centimetre graph paper, rubber-based glue, black pen.

1. Cut four sheets of paper 24 cm × 21·5 cm. Copy this Mayan sowing maize on to graph paper, then trace him on to cartridge paper.

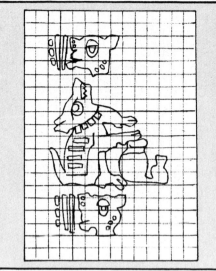

2. Dogs sing and beat drums in a religious ceremony, with the glyph or symbol for the rain-bird either side of them. Copy and trace this design, which is repeated four times, on the second page of your book.

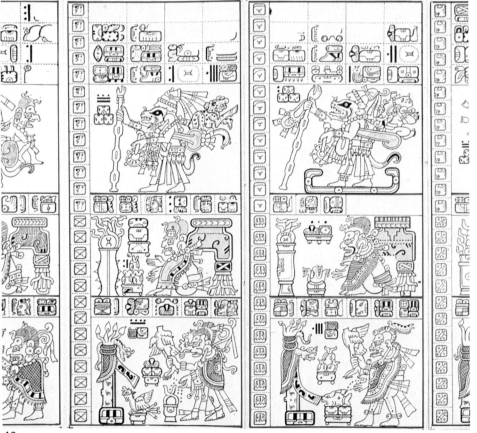

6. Measure and cut four pieces of stiff card 31·5 cm × 25·5 cm. This will give a firm backing to your illustrations. Put two sheets side by side and join with sticky tape. Fold the sheets together and put another strip of sticky tape down the spine. Do the same with the other two sheets.

3. The star gods, such as this Venus god, were important to the Mayans. Shown here hurling a spear, the Venus god was also the patron of hunters. This illustration will go on to the third page of your folding book.

4. You can end your book with a decorative illustration based on various Mayan glyphs (the rectangle stands for the first month of the year) and designs. This illustration will go on to the fourth page of the book.

5. Paint the illustrations with thick poster paints. You may copy the colours shown here or choose your own. When the paint is dry, outline the drawings with a black pen.

7. Join the two pairs of sheets with sticky tape, as shown. Glue your illustrations on to the card.

8. You can add as many pages as you want to your finished folding book and, of course, use the real folding books to help you design your own story.

The Minotaur

Angry glances were thrown at the dark-skinned Minoans as they strode arrogantly up and down the streets of ancient Athens in Greece. Impatiently, Prince Theseus asked his father why he did not defy them. But his father only shook his head and muttered that his son's impatience would be the death of him. Theseus spun on his heel and walked down into the market-place where the young men and women were lining up so that the Minoans could select their quota. Theseus slipped into the ranks. When the Minoan officer reached Theseus, he pushed him into the centre of the square with six other boys and seven girls.

Within minutes, the Athenians had been bundled on board a Minoan warship. Three days later, the ship anchored in a superb harbour near Knossos, the capital of the island of Crete in the Aegean Sea. The young people disembarked and were marched off to the royal prison.

Not for the first time, Theseus wondered angrily what had possessed him to join the line-up in Athens. As he glowered at the ground, the door swung back with a crash and an officer announced that Ariadne, the king's daughter, would now select the chosen ones to be sacrificed to the Minotaur.

The Greeks were herded, blinking, into the bright sunshine of the prison courtyard. At one end, attended by priestesses, was a beautiful girl, the daughter of King Minos. The prisoners were paraded before her. As Theseus feared, he was among those selected. Then, Ariadne descended from her throne and approached them. As the king's daughter drew level with him, she stopped and, to the horror of her attendants, asked him where he came from. Before he knew it, Theseus was telling her his whole history. At length she turned shyly away and left him with a pleasant word of farewell.

During the next nine days,

Theseus had watched his companions being led away to he knew not what, and now it was his turn. The cell door swung open and an officer beckoned. After they had made their way through a maze of corridors, the officer stopped and pushed Theseus through a doorway. The door clanged shut behind him and he was alone in complete darkness.

As he stood waiting for his eyes to become accustomed to the dim light, a figure carrying a burning torch slipped out of the shadows. It was Ariadne. Breathlessly, she handed him the torch, a sword and a ball of string, one end of which she had tied to a pillar. Before he could ask any questions, she had whispered, 'Beware!' and was gone. As Theseus wandered through the labyrinth of passages, paying out the thread, he was aware of an overpowering sense of menace. Suddenly, there was an ear-splitting bellow of rage and there before him stood a hideous monster, half man and half bull. The Minotaur rushed at Theseus, roaring savagely. Instinctively, Theseus thrust his sword forward to protect himself and the bull-man was impaled upon its blade.

Almost unable to believe his luck, Theseus started to make his way back through the labyrinth, winding in the thread as he went. At the door to the maze, he found Ariadne waiting for him. Without a pause or a word of explanation, she led him through the silent palace and the streets of the capital to the harbour where a ship was waiting. Soon, they were at sea with the outline of Crete fast disappearing in the moonlit distance. Bewildered, Theseus turned to Ariadne and asked her why she had helped him. Softly, she replied, 'You must ask the gods'.

Right: The Minotaur prepares to hurl himself upon Prince Theseus, not knowing that he is armed and ready for battle.

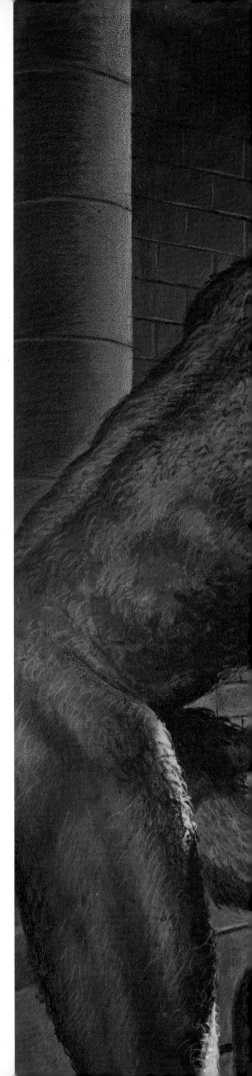

The Palace of Knossos

Above: The remains of Knossos are located near the modern capital of Crete, Heraklion.

Above: Sir Arthur Evans, who excavated Knossos, holds the bull's head he found there.

Was there ever a King Minos, a Theseus, an Ariadne and, most important of all, a Minotaur? In the 1890s, a rich Englishman, Arthur Evans, suspected he had discovered mysterious *hieroglyphs* of an ancient civilization in Crete. Evans called the founders of the civilization the Minoans, in memory of the legendary King Minos.

His most exciting find was the Palace of Knossos in 1900. This vast complex, the later part of which is dated to around 1500 to 1450 B.C., covered no less than three hectares. Indeed, the term 'palace' may be misleading as Knossos contained a vast number of offices, stores full of *amphorae* for wine and olive oil, workshops and sacred shrines as well as a host of state rooms. The palace had been a vast labyrinth full of soldiers, civil servants, storekeepers and craftsmen as well as the royal family and the nobility.

The palace was built around a huge inner courtyard. The buildings rose several storeys high and were made of perfectly shaped stones. An absolute maze of corridors linked the different parts of the palace. They and the inner rooms were lit by great openings in the ceiling. The state rooms were approached from an imposing grand staircase.

Evans was particularly impressed by what he took to be the throne room. Against one wall stood a magnificent sculptured stone throne. In the middle of the room there was a sunken area where he believed the Minoan king made ritual ceremonies of purification. Further away, he discovered a suite of rooms which he believed had belonged to the king. One of the most exciting was the Hall of the Double Axes. This was decorated not only with the sign of the double axe, but also with great figure-of-eight shields. Another group of rooms, which may have belonged to the queen, included a hall decorated with dolphins and a bathroom including a marble hip-bath and a flush toilet.

What were the people like who lived in these rooms? A series of beautiful wall paintings provides the answer. The ladies of the court were heavily made up and wore tight bodices and bell-like crinoline skirts. The courtiers lounged about in loincloths or short trousers with wide belts around their waists. The women's hair was elaborately

46

curled and decorated with combs and the men's hair was decorated with feather head-dresses.

But where was the labyrinth? Although Evans searched everywhere, he could not find any sign of a great network of underground tunnels. What he did find, however, was a sophisticated system of flood drains and sewers. Could it be that earlier visitors to Crete thought that these tunnels were some kind of maze?

What of the Minotaur? Evans came across the remains of a fine wall painting or *fresco* showing a young man in the act of somersaulting over the back of an enormous charging bull. A young girl was waiting to steady him when he landed. It seems that the ancient Minoans enjoyed either some kind of bull-fighting or gymnastic displays in which huge bulls were used as vaulting horses!

Bulls seemed to have played a great part in the Minoans' religious life. Superb bulls' heads were carved out of *steatite* or *soapstone* and fitted with horns made of wood painted in gold. It may be that the ancient rulers of Crete appeared before their people on ceremonial occasions wearing a hollowed-out bull's head and that this gave rise to the legend of the Minotaur.

Theseus and his companions may well represent real hostages who were collected from the Greek cities that formed part of the Minoan empire. Certainly, there is ample evidence that the Minoans were a great sea power, although they do not seem to have occupied the Greek islands and mainland.

Some archaeologists believe that the story of Theseus and the Minotaur really explains in romantic terms the sudden and unexplained collapse of the Minoan empire. Did Greek invaders raid Knossos, kill King Minos and carry off the fair Ariadne? Or did the great bull that, according to the Minoans, lived beneath Crete rise up in rage and destroy the civilization with an earthquake?

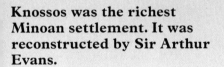

Knossos was the richest Minoan settlement. It was reconstructed by Sir Arthur Evans.

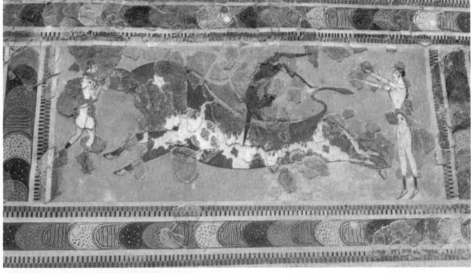

Above: This fresco from Knossos shows bull-leaping, a favourite Minoan sport.

Below: Water from these drains at Knossos led to sewers below, thought to be the labyrinth.

Mazes and Labyrinths

Start

Passage to

escape tunnel

Labyrinths and mazes have always fascinated people. We know that labyrinths, underground buildings with many passages and rooms, were built about 2500 years ago in ancient Egypt.

In gardening, a labyrinth or maze has an intricate system of pathways enclosed with thick hedges. In the simplest kind of maze, which has one entrance and exit, the idea is to find the centre and then the way out. This may be done by placing one hand against either wall and keeping it there until one has been round the whole maze.

Battle of the labyrinth

Re-enact Theseus's fight with the Minotaur in the labyrinth! This game (right) is for two players. You will need two dice and two moving pieces (you can either use counters or copy the illustrations of the Minotaur and Theseus on to thin card). The player who throws the highest score can choose which character he or she will play. If Theseus reaches the escape tunnel (he must make an exact throw to do this) without being 'caught' by the Minotaur, that player is the winner. The Minotaur wins if he lands on the same square as Theseus. Players who land on any of the squares in the passage to the tunnel may move backwards or forwards. The Minotaur cannot enter the escape tunnel.

Above: This coin came from the palace of Knossos on Crete. It shows an example of one of the simplest kinds of maze.

48

Start

King Solomon's Mines

In the Year of our Lord 1536, I, Alfonso Cabral, led a small expeditionary force from Sofala in East Africa. For years, we, the Portuguese, the greatest explorers in the world, have been trading with the lost land of Monomotapa.

From time to time, caravans reach the coast from the interior. They are led by dignified black chiefs, the tassels of whose skin robes sweep the ground as they walk. They carry short stabbing spears and bows and arrows in their hands and wear iron swords thrust into wooden scabbards, held together and decorated with gold and other metals.

We have found these tribesmen cunning traders who strike a hard bargain. In return for their gold, they demand our finest luxury goods: cloth, china and ornaments.

We have questioned them closely about their secret land and are sure it is where the mighty King Solomon obtained his gold, jewels and ivory from the queen of Sheba many centuries ago. The tribesmen told us much. Their land of Monomotapa is ruled by a rich and powerful king who lives in a great stone town called Zimbabwe. The town is dominated by an enormous castle, whose stones are so cunningly cut that they need no mortar to bind them together. The king lives in great state and is waited upon by hordes of servants who may only appear before him on bended knee.

The tribesmen assured us that their people are skilful farmers and produce good crops. As their weapons prove, they are expert metal workers and also make very fine pottery.

Questioning our guests as closely as we could, we learnt strange things about their king. Although truly powerful, the king of Monomotapa is unlike any European ruler in that he is completely subject to the law of the land. If the king is foolish enough to show more favour to one man than to another, he is deposed and replaced by a more impartial ruler.

We knew from the Arab merchants who dominated the trade of East Africa until we arrived that the people of Monomotapa had been trading in gold and jewels for hundreds of years. However, these Arabs had never succeeded in making their way to the lost empire. This we were determined to accomplish ourselves.

After the Monomotapans had finished trading, they packed up their camp and marched off into the interior. Giving them some hours' start, I sent off scouts to get as close to their rearguard as they could without being seen and to report the Africans' progress to me at regular intervals. Some hours later, I followed with an army of several hundred well-armed soldiers and a train of bearers.

At first all went well. Our scouts reported regularly and we made good time crossing the coastlands. But then our troubles began. Soon, we entered the densest forest we had ever seen.

In this terrifying jungle, poisonous snakes, hideous reptiles and sinking sands took their toll of lives, while fierce wild animals trapped the unwary. It was not long before my men succumbed to the fevers that haunt this dreadful land. Then, many men were killed by the little dark-skinned people of the jungle who came stealthily in the night. One morning, I found that all the bearers and scouts had fled, leaving us alone.

There was nothing for it but to return. As we retraced out steps to the coast, my army had dwindled to a handful of men. By the time I and my companions reached Sofala, we numbered but ten. Surely, the secrets of the land of Monomotapa will remain hidden for ever.

Right: The king of Zimbabwe receives African traders and exchanges gold for Portuguese cloth and Chinese porcelain.

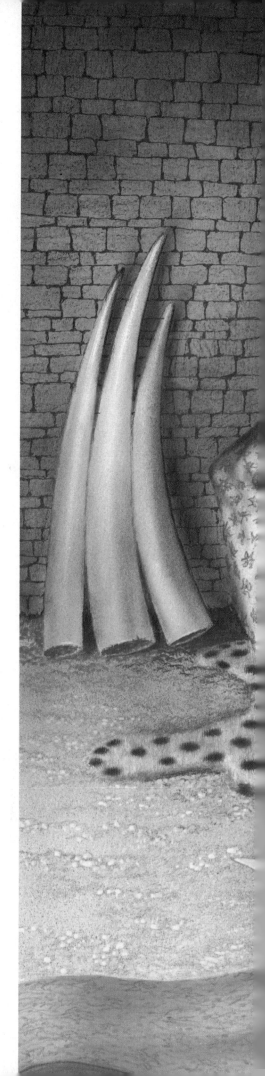

Great Zimbabwe

Above: The ruins of medieval Zimbabwe are situated in the centre of Zimbabwe-Rhodesia.

Great Zimbabwe is a group of stone ruins lying about 17 miles southeast of Fort Victoria in Zimbabwe-Rhodesia. There are great walls, rounded gateways, tall towers and a number of state buildings. On the top of a hill, there is a strong fort or citadel, which is called the Acropolis. On the plain below lies a great oval building called The Temple or the Great Enclosure.

All these buildings are made of flat, brick-like stones. The stones were chopped out of great leaves of granite which lie on the hillsides. The splendid buildings of Zimbabwe are made out of these stones which are piled one on top of another without any mortar or lime as a bond. Fine ironwork and pottery have been found near the ruins as well as a little gold and some beautiful soapstone birds.

The first Europeans who stumbled across the deserted ruins of Zimbabwe could not believe that such a large town could have been built by the ancestors of the simple black people who lived in the region. Karl Mauch, a German geologist who visited the ruins in 1871, spoke for most people when he declared that such a splendid town could only have been built by a civilized people in the distant past. In his opinion, the citadel was

Above: Great Zimbabwe covers a large area. This photograph shows the view from the hill ruins, with the large enclosure in the distance and the smaller ones in the foreground.

without doubt a copy of King Solomon's Temple, while the oval building was based on the palace the queen of Sheba lived in during her visit to Jerusalem in the tenth century B.C.

These ideas were accepted by most people until the beginning of the 20th century. As a result, treasure seekers started to ransack the ruins looking for gold. According to official records, no more than 14 kilograms of gold were ever found, but there is no saying how many precious objects were smuggled away and then melted down.

Mauch and the other archaeologists who followed his lead are known as the 'Phoenician School', as it was suggested that these famous traders from Tyre in Palestine were the founders of Zimbabwe. Other members of the group suggested that the master race came from ancient Egypt and still others believed that the civilizers came from ancient India.

On the other hand, there are those who form part of another school of thought called 'the Medievalists', who believe that the ruins are African in origin and medieval in date. In their opinion, Zimbabwe was built and rebuilt over many hundreds of years, the later part probably being constructed in the early 15th century. This group is led by David Randall-MacIver who examined the ruins in 1905. He pointed out that the only real difference between the houses erected by the Bantu in his day and those built by the people of Zimbabwe was in the materials used: the great soapstone birds of ancient Zimbabwe are very like modern Bantu lightning birds which are supposed to deceive the lightning and send it elsewhere during storms. He believed that the ruins were built during the Middle Ages because he found the remains of datable Chinese porcelain and Arab silver trade goods. Modern radio-carbon dating tests on wood

Above: The king may have lived in the 'Acropolis' in Zimbabwe.

Above: The Conical Tower in the large enclosure probably symbolized a grain bin.

Below: One of the soapstone 'thunder' birds of Zimbabwe.

from the Zimbabwean buildings have shown them to be medieval.

How civilized were the original inhabitants of Zimbabwe? Although the city was large and has yielded beads, clay pots, wire armlets and hoes, there is no sign of writing or of royal burial grounds. The early Zimbabweans seem to have enjoyed a simple Iron-Age culture and to have mined a little gold, but of King Solomon's Mines there is absolutely no sign.

What happened to Zimbabwe? Why was it deserted when Europeans first came across it? It seems that, between A.D. 500 and 1700, a series of black peoples occupied the city and its surrounding country. At its most powerful, Monomotapa included what is now Zimbabwe-Rhodesia and parts of Zaire, Mozambique and South Africa. Soon after 1700, however, a new warlike tribe, the Rozwe, arrived and destroyed the kingdom of Monomotapa. At some time after 1725, the Rozwe rebuilt Zimbabwe, which continued to prosper until about a century later when the Nguni took over. In the years that followed, barbarian invasions, continuous civil wars and the loss of their trade caused the people to desert their stone towns and forts and to return to being simple Iron-Age farmers. By the time the Europeans reached Zimbabwe the local people had forgotten everything about the early history of their country. It was as though the town had never existed.

Build an Ancient Settlement

In Great Zimbabwe, the king probably lived in the citadel or Acropolis. The Great Enclosure, which is also known as The Temple, is thought to have contained the impressive houses of either the royal wives or the most important tribespeople. Noblemen and their families would have lived in the smaller enclosures, the ruins of which you can see in the photograph on page 52.

These enclosures were divided into separate courtyards by stone walls and the circular houses themselves. The walls of the houses were built of clay, smoothed down to give a hard, even finish, and the roofs were thatched. A whole family would have lived in one of these enclosures. There were houses for the wives and children, for sleeping, cooking and for receiving guests. The rest of the people of Zimbabwe lived in much more cramped conditions in huts outside the walls of the enclosures.

Above: Huts similar to the ones being constructed above were built within the smaller stone enclosures at Great Zimbabwe, the ruins of which you can see in the photograph on page 52. Here the men are putting together the basic framework of a hut which will be covered later with clay.

Build an enclosure

You will need: newspaper, modelling clay or plasticine, modelling tool, rolling pin, thin card, straws, poster paint, paintbrush, scissors, pencil, compass, sticks, string, paper-clips, sticky tape, clear glue.

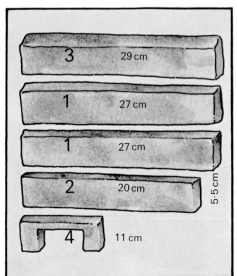

4. Roll out four thick strips of clay to make sections of the wall as shown, using two sticks as a guide. Roll out one shorter strip 11 cm long and cut out a shape to form the doorway. (The numbers on each section correspond to those on the photograph of the finished model on the opposite page.)

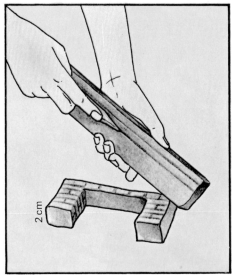

5. Smooth the edges of each section of wall and score grooves in each one with a modelling tool to make a brick pattern.

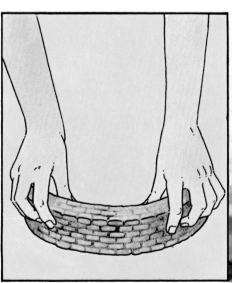

6. Bend each section of the wall into shape while the clay is still soft, following the layout of the model in the photograph on the opposite page.

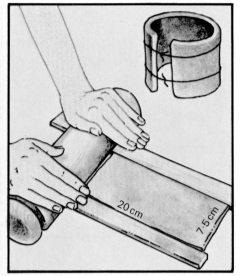

1. Roll out a thin sheet of clay 20 cm × 7·5 cm. While still quite soft, bend into the shape of a hut, leaving an opening for the door. To keep the clay in shape while drying, carefully tie two pieces of string around it. Repeat these instructions for the second hut.

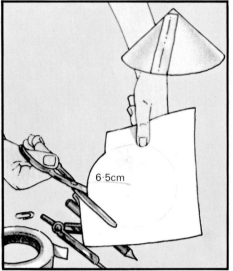

2. For the roof, draw a circle 13 cm in diameter on to thin card. Cut out, make a slit to the centre and fold round into a cone shape. Hold the opening together with a paper-clip, then fasten with sticky tape on the outside and inside. Repeat for the second roof.

3. Cut straws to size and flatten one end of each straw. Stick the straws firmly to the roof shape with the flat ends in the centre, until the roof is completely covered. Paint and leave to dry.

7. Lay out the small enclosure as shown in the photograph. Where the sections of the wall meet, put a small stick to act as a join.

8. You can add small plants or models of people and animals to your enclosure.

The Sacrifice

It was a cold, bitter cold day, 2000 years ago. An icy wind whipped thick, dull grey clouds across the sky. A group of people stood huddled together near a gnarled and broken tree. On one side of them, the great marsh of Tollund Fen in Jutland stretched away into the distance. As the wind whistled through the tall dry rushes, the people retreated from the tree leaving a lonely, upright figure. He was a noble-looking man of just above middle height, with cropped hair and a closely shaven face.

For a moment he turned and looked yearningly towards a small village of longhouses. He had spent many happy years there. He could imagine the scene in his longhouse with its warm, dark atmosphere filled with the smell of smoked meat and stored vegetables, although there was little enough of these. The women would be bustling about preparing the meal, the old people squatting near the fire and the youngsters rolling and fighting in the rushes on the floor.

Last year had been a hard one, the hardest he had ever known. The summer had been wet and cold and the crops grown in the little rectangular fields close to the houses had been poor. The harvest had been reaped wet and much of it had spoiled. Most of what was left had to be kept for planting the next year. Disease had spread among the cattle and many had to be slaughtered. Even the wild fruits had been fewer than usual.

The winter had been unusually cold with plentiful falls of snow. The sea had frozen over so that fishing, one of the village's main sources of food, became impossible. When the ice melted, there had been raging storms in which several of their frail fishing vessels had sunk. This meant that the village had an unusually large number of widows and orphans to look after.

No, the good days were gone. The gods were angry. There could be no other explanation for their run of bad luck. Witchcraft might have been the cause if there had been only a few disasters, but no witch had the power to bring the whole village to the verge of starvation. So, the sacrifice was necessary.

Sadly, he thought of his wife. Fortunately, their sons would look after their mother. Not that she would need much help, once the shock had worn off. She had always been a strong woman and had helped him through many a bad year, but never one like the last.

Slightly shivering in the cold wind, he looked around him for the last time at the bleak scene. Above him, he watched a bird soaring free. For a moment, he stood motionless until the bird disappeared out of sight. Then, he stripped off his woollen trousers, his fur-lined coat and shirt and stood naked except for a leather girdle around his waist and a tight leather cap on his head. When he was ready, two men stepped forward from the little group and lifted him carefully, reverently, until he could slip his head inside the leather noose which hung from the old broken tree. On his signal, the men released their grip and left their lord and master dangling from the rope.

There was no struggle. He gave his life willingly, lovingly for his people. When it was over, they cut down his body and gently bent his arms and legs until he lay like a child in the womb. Then, very carefully, they lifted his body and carried it to the swamp. After laying it upon the soft peat, they watched it sink slowly beneath the surface of the cold brown water. To the last they could see the same calm smile upon his face. Then, he was gone. All that they could do now was wait and see if the gods accepted the sacrifice. They prayed that it had not been in vain.

Right: The village elder of Tollund prepares to sacrifice himself for his people's good.

The Peat Bog Murder Mystery

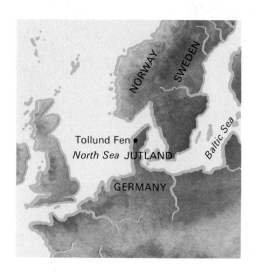

Above: Tollund man was found in a peat bog in the centre of Jutland, now modern Denmark.

Below: The 2000-year-old body of Tollund Man shortly after its removal from the bog.

On a dull day in May 1950, two farmers were cutting peat for their fires in a bog in Bjaeldskov Valley, Tollund Fen, in what was formerly Jutland but is now part of Denmark. As they skilfully cut and lifted slabs of peat, they saw a face looking up at them. Filled with horror, they cleared the peat away from the body and lifted it out on to the side of the bog. The body was crouching with arms and legs bent and its head was bowed forward. The dead man wore a cap made of pieces of hide sewn together, secured under the chin with a leather strap. A smooth leather belt was bound round his waist. He wore no other clothes. His hair had been cut very short and he had been clean shaven, although there was a light stubble all over his jaws as his beard had

continued to grow for a short time after death. The man appeared to have been strangled as there was a thin leather noose around his neck.

The farmers made their way as quickly as they could to a telephone and contacted the police. They informed the police that they had recovered what appeared to be a murder victim from Tollund Fen. To their surprise the police did not seem to be very disturbed by their news and asked a number of questions about the state of the body. As soon as the police had finished the call, they contacted their local museum and asked if one of the curators could accompany them to the scene of the crime. This was not the first body to be recovered from the Danish bogs and the police were taking no chances. After a brief examination,

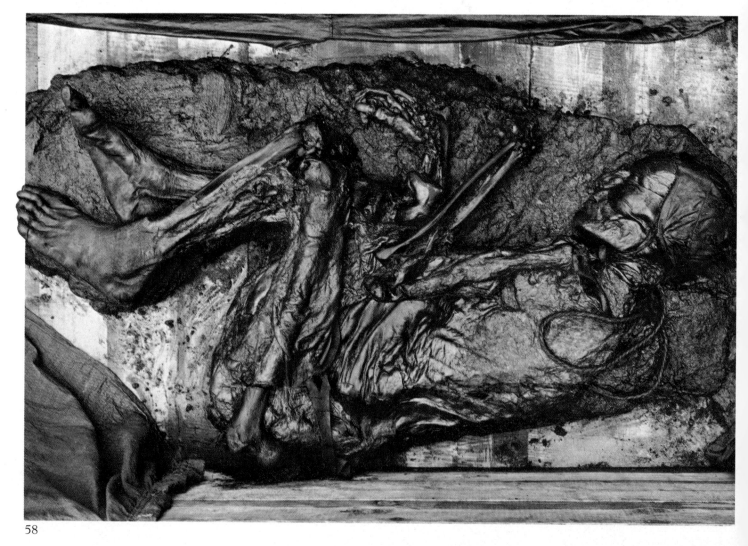

the museum experts confirmed their suspicions: the body was of ancient origin.

Tollund Man, as he came to be known, was immediately moved to the National Museum in Copenhagen so that he could be studied before his body disintegrated. Examination of the block of peat where the body had been found suggested that Tollund Man had been thrown into the bog about 2000 years previously. The *bog* water, which was full of soil acids, had marvellously preserved the body. The experts could tell that he was over 20 years of age when he died because his wisdom teeth had come through. A full examination of his brain, heart and the rest of his organs showed that he had enjoyed good health up until the time of his death. The stomach contained the remains of his last meal which was probably a bowl of gruel made from barley, linseed, knotweed and many other herbs. From its half-digested state, the scientists could tell that he had not eaten for between 12 and 24 hours before his death.

What remained to be discovered was what had happened to Tollund Man. There were several possible explanations for his presence in the bog. He could have committed suicide by hanging or he could have been murdered. He might have been hanged for committing a serious crime. He might have been executed as a prisoner of war. Finally, he might have been offered as a sacrifice to the gods. Hanging, as we know from Roman writings, was regarded as an honourable form of execution among the ancient German tribes. On the other hand, criminals were also executed by being drowned in bogs. Moreover, prisoners of war seem to have been killed in this way. However, if Tollund Man had been a prisoner of war, the archaeologists would have expected to have found some more bodies or at least some weapons buried in the same area. A

Above: Tollund Man must have lived in a village very much like this reconstructed one.

Below: A reconstruction of the interior of an Iron-Age house with the traditional fire-pit.

careful search was made but yielded no more evidence.

Most archaeologists feel that the likeliest explanation of Tollund Man's death is that he was sacrificed to the gods. He died during the winter, when food was in short supply. By sacrificing one of their senior men, the Bog People may have hoped to please the gods.

However, the famous archaeologist, Sir Mortimer Wheeler, gave a rather different explanation in 1955 after eating an exact copy of Tollund Man's last meal. Taking a good swig of brandy, to get rid of the rather unpleasant taste of the food, he announced, 'Tollund Man probably committed suicide to escape his wife's cooking!'

Solve a Murder

Here is a chance to try your hand at being a detective! Imagine that you are an archaeologist and, after reading the evidence below, see if you can answer all the questions that follow.

The evidence
The body was discovered by peat-cutters several metres below the surface of a Danish bog. The head, body and limbs were perfectly preserved. There was a short leather noose around the man's neck, and he was wearing the remains of a sheepskin cape, woollen trousers and leather boots. Lying beside his head was a sturdy leather helmet, and a sword and spear-head were discovered close to the body.

On examining the body, scientists found that the victim's wisdom teeth had not come through and that the molars were not badly ground down. X-rays of the skull showed that the suture lines (where the bones meet) were still visible.

Careful study of the limbs disclosed marks on the wrists and ankles which could have been made by a rope found beside the body. The man's nails were broken and there were fragments of someone else's skin under them. The man's arms were behind his back.

Several long scars were found on the victim's body which had healed well before his death. His stomach was full of half-digested food including barley, rye, raspberries, buttercups, wild camomile and many small fragments of animal flesh and bone.

A small silver ring was found on the fourth finger of his right hand and a handsome bronze brooch on his cape.

Right: Look carefully at this illustration of a body found in a peat bog. You will find some of the clues you need to answer the questions on the next page.

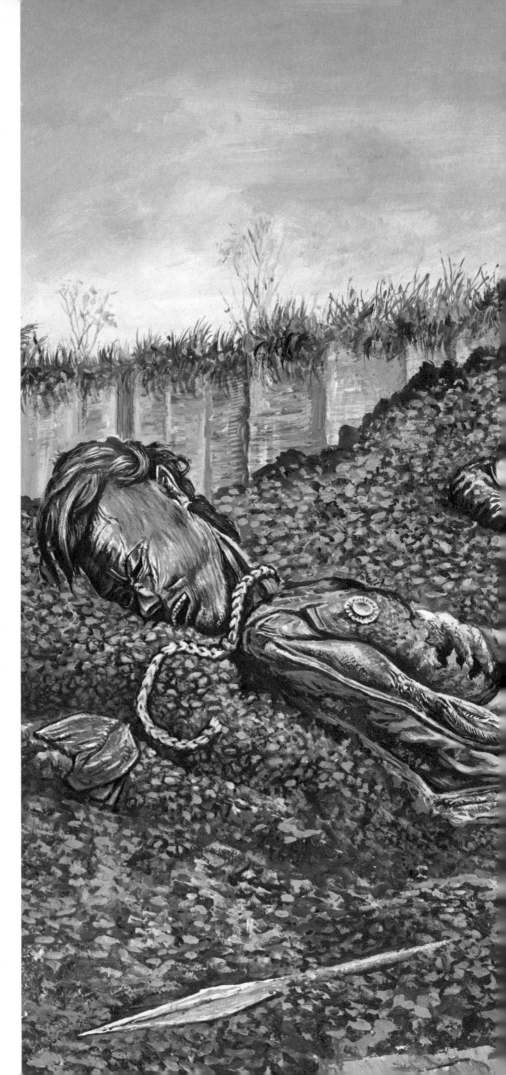

The questions

You may give as many reasons for your answers as you can.

1. How do you think the victim met his death?

2. What makes you think that he did not go voluntarily to his death?

3. How old do you think the victim was at the time of his death?

4. What type of work do you think he did for a living?

5. What kind of meal did he have immediately before his death?

6. How long before his death had he eaten his last meal?

7. In which season of the year did he die?

8. Do you think the victim was poor or rich?

How to tell a body's age

This information may help you answer the questions:

The rear molar or wisdom teeth usually come through between the 17th and 25th year.

When the skull has completed its growth, which is usually by the 15th year, the seams or sutures between the skull bones gradually disappear and the skull becomes one continuous bony shell.

The answers

1. The man was probably hanged (there was a leather noose around his neck).

2. There were marks on his wrists and ankles.

3. We know he was a young man because he had no wisdom teeth and the suture lines in the skull were visible.

4. He was a soldier (there were weapons found by him and he had scars on his body).

5. A meat and vegetable stew.

6. Twelve to 24 hours (the food in his stomach was half-digested).

7. In the summer (there were remains of raspberries in his stomach).

8. He was rich because he wore a silver ring and a bronze brooch.

The Nazca

One day, early in the seventh century, the triumphant Nazca army marched through the streets of their capital, Cahuachi, past the High Priest. The chiefs swaggered in their embroidered tunics, turbans and elaborate sandals, and their elegant cloaks swung in the breeze. Their faces were painted bright colours and they wore gold ear and nose rings, necklaces and bracelets. Behind them marched their tired warriors carrying long-handled, heavy-headed maces and wide-bladed knives. This advance guard was followed by men bearing the trophies of war. There were hundreds of severed heads as well as piles of gold ornaments and weapons. Behind them came the prisoners, their heads bowed, ignoring the jeers of the crowd.

Once the parade was over and the priests had offered some of the prisoners to the gods, the Nazca people gave themselves up to feasting and dancing while a small party kept guard over the remaining prisoners. As soon as the celebrations were over, bodies of the Nazca who had been killed in battle were carried to the city of the dead, where tombs were cut out of solid rock six metres below ground. Each of these graves had room for several bodies. The chiefs were arranged in a sitting position in woven baskets. In addition to their weapons and ornaments, they were equipped for the next life with magnificent feather cloaks and fans.

While the dead and wounded were being cared for, the prisoners of war were set to work on the land. The Nazca were fine farmers and made use of every centimetre of earth they could find. Soon, the prisoners were building stone retaining walls along the hillsides and spreading soil over the new terraces. These flat strips were planted with maize, beans and squash. Some of the prisoners helped to repair the aqueducts, which carried life-giving water down from the mountains to the

network of *irrigation* canals which spread it over the fields. Others helped the Nazca to manure the ground with rich *guano* fertilizer, and to water and weed the plants on their terraces.

Once this had been done it was time for the most important task of all. The Nazca and their prisoners made their way to the desert, where they found that the priests had already marked out the sacred lines for them to follow. For hours prisoner and free citizen alike toiled in the blazing sun, clearing the desert and deepening the lines. Piles of heavy stones were collected from the desert and arranged beside the sacred marks. The prisoners were clearly puzzled, not knowing what these lines were for. But what to the ignorant were simple lines in the desert were superb drawings and sacred designs to the gods in the heavens. They could look down from above the clouds and enjoy their people's handiwork. In addition, the priests used them to work out their calendar.

It was now midsummer, and all the Nazca people left their small, dried-brick villages and made their way to the capital to celebrate the renewal of the Sun. Past the royal palace and the temple-towers, they marched to the Place of Stakes where the sacred rites were performed. Here among the standing wooden pillars they gave praise to the god who, above all others, held their future in his hands. No sacrifice was too great for him. By the evening, the altars on the temple-pyramids were running with the blood of the last of the prisoners of war. It was soon time to launch another attack upon one of the neighbouring tribes if the Nazca people were to keep the gods satisfied.

Right: A Nazca High Priest prays to his gods at sunset before the drawing of a giant spider, traced on the desert floor of the great Nazca plain.

Lines in the Desert

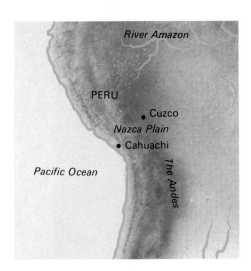

Above: The Nazca lived in the plains and valleys of what is now the southern part of Peru.

In the vast, stony deserts of Peru, there is a mystery which still puzzles archaeologists. In a valley belonging to a tributary of the Rio Grande river, Paul Kosok, a lecturer from Long Island University in the United States, discovered in 1941 what he took to be the remains of an ancient irrigation system. As he studied these lines from the air, he realized that many of them were gigantic drawings. There were enormous birds and animals and even a giant spider. In addition to the drawings there was a large number of intricate designs which he called roads. Some are in the form of zigzags, others are spirals and others geometric shapes.

Closer study showed that people had cut shallow furrows in the desert and lined them with stones. It was easy enough to see how ancient artists had made these lines, but how did they manage to draw them to such a large scale that they could only be appreciated from the air? However, if one is a good artist, it is not an impossible task to mark out really large shapes on the ground. Moreover, researchers have found the remains of wooden stakes which appear to have been used as markers by the ancient Nazca artists.

The question, 'Who made the lines?' is somewhat easier. The drawings in the Nazca Valley and Plain are associated with prehistoric burials and ruins in the same area containing vividly painted pottery, fine cloth and basketwork which date from between 200 B.C. and A.D. 600. Radio-carbon dating tests carried out on samples taken from the wooden stakes used in the construction of the drawings have yielded dates of A.D. 550 to 610.

The really puzzling question is why the Nazca people went to the trouble of making these lines in the desert. It was thought that it would have taken large numbers of people an enormous amount of time to produce these wonders. Experiments in building such designs in the desert have shown, however, that they can be produced by people who know what they are doing in relatively short periods of time. Nevertheless the drawings must have represented a very considerable effort by a large proportion of their not very large population. There must have been very compelling reasons for their puzzling behaviour.

It has been suggested that the Nazca lines, like so many ancient monuments, may have been the ruler's way of controlling his subjects' behaviour. As long as the people were completely absorbed

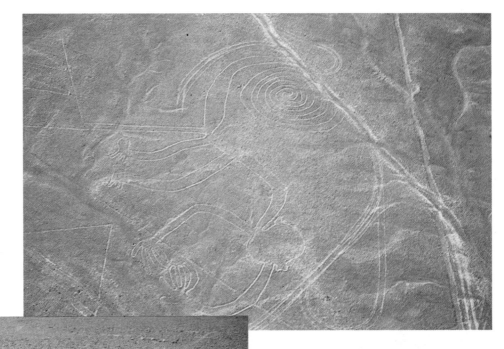

Left: Lines traced in the Nazca desert vanish into the distance. Some archaeologists and astronomers believe the lines mark the positions of the sun and stars during the year and formed a giant calendar.

Right: This drawing of a monkey may represent the Plough, whose movements told the Nazca when to expect the flood waters.

Below: This photograph shows the size of the Nazca drawings. The woman is standing by the monkey's tail.

Below: The Nazca people preserved the bodies of their dead by *mummifying* them.

with their work on these massive enterprises, they would not question their ruler's decisions or demand better living conditions.

Some archaeologists believe that the drawings were elaborate offerings to the gods and that this is the reason that they can only be appreciated from above the Earth. They would point out that the Nazca are not the only people to make giant drawings. The prehistoric people of southern Britain, for example, carved the shapes of men and horses out of the chalk on the sides of hills in Kent and Wiltshire. The American Indians traced giant pictures in the deserts of North America.

Many of the lines seem to mark the position of the sun during different periods of the year as well as the rising and setting of some important stars and planets. Although astronomers have studied the designs carefully, they have not been able to prove beyond doubt whether the lines form a prehistoric calendar or not. Certainly, such knowledge would have been extremely useful because the people could have calculated which was the best time to sow their crops, and so on. However, the need for such knowledge does not prove that the Nazca had found a way of discovering it. Moreover, many of the lines do not fit into any known

astronomical pattern.

Perhaps our greatest chance of finding a logical explanation is to study peoples who lived close to the Nazca. The ancient Incas, one of the most powerful and successful of the South American peoples, also constructed a series of lines and shrines from their capital Cuzco. Every day of the year, a different group of city dwellers worshipped at a particular shrine on a specific line. It seems as if the whole valley was divided up into a series of pilgrimage routes. The capital city itself was laid out in the shape of a puma. It may be, therefore, that the Nazca lines, like the Inca lines, are part of a religious calendar.

65

Design Your Own Nazca Drawing

As you have read, archaeologists have not been able to discover what the huge animal figures and puzzling lines in the Nazca desert really mean. However, one possible solution is that these drawings, such as the one of the spider, represent constellations of stars, something like our own signs of the zodiac. The movements of all these stars in particular seem to have enabled the Nazca priests to predict the dates when the mountain flood waters would reach the plains. This would have been of great help in planning the sowing and irrigation of crops. Even today, farmers in the Andes Mountains in Peru work out when to sow their seeds and harvest their crops by studying the stars.

Below: This drawing of a hummingbird, seen here in an aerial photograph, may represent one of the signs of the zodiac.

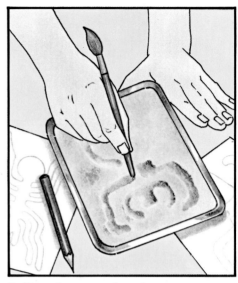

You will need: sand (if possible, two different colours, if not, imitation tarmac, obtainable from a model shop, or fine gravel or rice may be used for the second colour), small box (or plant tray or tin lid), paintbrush.
1. Fill the box with sand and dampen this with water.

2. Practise your drawing on paper first. Copy any of the Nazca line drawings in the photographs, or follow the insect design shown here. With the end of the paintbrush, draw the design carefully on to the sand, making a groove to take the second colour.

3. Make a pouring cone from a circle of paper, leaving a hole just big enough to let your second colour sand trickle through. Fill the cone with sand or imitation tarmac and carefully fill in the design.

4. You can also obtain a good effect by using fine gravel or rice (or lentils!) to draw in your design.

5. Gently brush any surplus sand away from the design with a paintbrush.

6. Try to use two different colours which contrast strongly, as this will make the drawing stand out more clearly.

Vinland

Thorfinn Karlsefni stared proudly at his three *longships*. Broader and deeper than his people's warships, these 'Ocean-striding Bisons' slid through the water and were perfect for deep-sea sailing.

Who would have thought a few years ago that he would be leading an expedition of 160 men and women to Vinland? Twenty years before, Leif Eriksson had been the first to winter in the new land probably known later as Newfoundland. Then, after only two years, his brother, Thorvold, had led another expedition there. Unfortunately, this voyage had ended tragically as Thorvold had been killed by the local people, the Skraelings, as Thorvold's men called them. In spite of this, Thorfinn had had little difficulty assembling a group of settlers some 20 years later. Now at last everything was ready and the cattle led protesting on board.

The voyage from Greenland went exactly according to plan. The settlers followed Leif Eriksson's instructions and reached his stopping-over place in Vinland. They repaired the huts he had left and settled down to sit out the winter. This was long and bitterly cold and food was short.

When the ice melted at last, some had had enough and voted to return to Greenland. Sadly, Thorfinn agreed and the disgruntled families sailed for home. The rest, however, sailed south until they reached a land-locked bay which they named Hope. The bay was protected by large sandbanks which could only be crossed at high tide. The broad calm river that ran into it was full of fine, fat fish. Just beyond the shore, they found wild wheat growing. The nearby woods were full of fur-bearing animals which provided both food and clothing. Overjoyed, the settlers felt their troubles were over and started building a settlement.

Early one morning, there was a cry of warning from the lookout.

Thorfinn rushed to the shore and, shading his eyes, stared at a fleet of little wooden boats. The paddlers were dark-skinned men with long black hair. As they approached they chanted and shook rattles. Thorfinn ordered his men to arm themselves but to offer no violence to their visitors. The Skraelings paddled up and down for some time. Then, apparently satisfied, they left.

For the rest of the summer and autumn, the settlers spent their time harvesting wild wheat and fruits. The cattle flourished in the rich pastures. The winter, when it came, was much milder than they could have hoped.

In the spring, the Skraelings returned but made it clear by signs that they only wanted to trade. At first, all went well and the settlers exchanged some of their red cloth for the Indians' furs. But then the Indians seemed interested in their weapons and became angry when they refused to sell them. Just at that moment the bull took it into his head to come rushing out of the forest and to start bellowing at the top of his voice. The Skraelings were terrified and fled to their boats and paddled away in haste.

It was hoped that would be the last they would see of the local people, but only three weeks later another fleet appeared. This time the Skraelings were determined to make war and charged the settlers as soon as they had beached their boats. As the battle swayed back and forth the settlers were saved by a woman called Freydis who dashed into battle to help her menfolk. For some reason this terrified the Skraelings who took to their boats.

Unfortunately, this experience was too much for the settlers who feared to suffer the fate of poor Thorvold. So, after all their work and in spite of the richness of the land, they returned to Greenland. Vinland was not for them.

Right: Indians attack the Viking settlement in Vinland.

The Vikings in America

Above: The Viking settlement found at L'Anse-aux-Meadows is on Newfoundland.

Did the Vikings ever reach America? For many years historians refused to believe that this was possible. There was, of course, no doubt that they had discovered and settled in Iceland and Greenland, because there is firm historical and archaeological evidence. But what evidence was there that the Vikings had ever reached America? The *sagas* or Icelandic histories which contained the accounts were vague and had been passed down by word of mouth for generations before being written down. Many historians dismissed them as vague imaginings. On the other hand, a German historian called Adam of Bremen described in 1075 how the king of the Danes had told him of a great island that had been discovered in the middle of the Atlantic Ocean. This island was called Wineland as grapes grew wild there. Although this was not the hard evidence wanted, it was a little more promising.

For many years, professional and amateur archaeologists scoured North America for evidence of a Viking landfall. In 1898, a Swedish-born farmer called Olaf Ohman found, or claimed to have found, a large stone bearing an inscription in Viking letters or *runes* about three miles from Kensington

in Minnesota. The inscription described how thirty Vikings had taken part in a voyage of exploration to Vinland in 1362. However, the inscription was shown to be a clumsy forgery.

Later, more eager amateur archaeologists in Minnesota claimed to have found some Viking *halberds* and battle-axes. The weapons on investigation turned out to be tobacco cutters! In 1930, the discovery of a genuine Viking sword and axe at Beardmore near Lake Nipigon in Ontario gave the experts hope. But once again they were disappointed because the weapons had been planted by a collector of Norse antiquities.

Then, in 1965, Yale University in the U.S.A. proudly announced that they had proof that the existence of America was known during the Middle Ages. The proof was the so-called Vinland Map which some experts claim to have been made in 1440. If genuine, this map would have proved that Europeans knew about America

Below: Detailed excavation takes place at the Viking site at L'Anse-aux-Meadows.

Above: The Vinland Map seemed to prove that the Vikings got to America before Colombus.

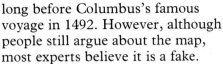

long before Columbus's famous voyage in 1492. However, although people still argue about the map, most experts believe it is a fake.

For a long time it seemed as if there would never be any definite archaeological evidence that the Vikings reached America. Then, in 1960, a Norwegian archaeologist called Helge Ingstad discovered a promising site at L'Anse-aux-Meadows in northern Newfoundland in Canada. A stone's throw from the sea, Dr Ingstad uncovered the ruins of two great houses closely resembling Viking dwellings found in Greenland. The bigger of the two houses was about 21 metres long and 17 metres wide. The floors were made of hard pressed clay, the walls of turf and the roof of timber and turf. In the centre of the house there was a fire-pit, and raised earth benches ran along the sides. Six to eight square living rooms were grouped round the central hall.

Besides the two halls and several smaller houses, there were the

Above: This North American Indian arrowhead was found in a Viking cemetery in Greenland.

remains of a *sauna* bath, a smithy and stables. Dr Ingstad believes that between 75 and 90 people lived there. Charred roof timbers have been dated by radio-carbon dating tests to about 1060, which is close to the traditional date given to the Viking voyages to Vinland in the sagas. The absence of runic inscriptions and the small number of Viking objects found, however, have caused some archaeologists to reject Dr Ingstad's claims.

On the other hand, there is a piece of evidence that links the Vikings to the North American Indians. In 1930, Aage Roussel found an ancient Indian arrowhead in the Viking churchyard at Sandnes in west Greenland. The arrowhead is made of a rock (a particular type of *quartzite*) which is only found in Labrador in North America. An almost identical arrowhead was discovered in an ancient Indian settlement by the Northwest River, Newfoundland, in 1956.

As you can see, although it has not been proved beyond all reasonable doubt that the Vikings reached America, it is extremely likely that they did so. However, the location of the actual places visited by Viking explorers and settlers is still a mystery.

Below: This reconstruction of a house interior shows how the Vikings may have lived.

Below: Thorfinn Karlsefni lived in this part of Iceland on his return from Vinland.

How to make a Viking Hall

Although some archaeologists are still not convinced that Dr Ingstad had discovered two genuine Viking halls or longhouses at L'Anse-aux-Meadows in Newfoundland, there is no doubt that the remains are very similar to those of recognized Viking halls found in Iceland and Greenland.

The fact that a small smithy was found at L'Anse-aux-Meadows with, amongst other things, scraps of worked iron, a stone anvil and a fire-pit, is very important. At that time, neither the Indians nor the Eskimos were capable of metal working, so it does seem extremely likely that L'Anse-aux-Meadows was indeed a Viking settlement.

You will need: balsa-wood: 2·88 m × 1 cm × 1 cm (base, roof supports, crossbeams and rafters); corrugated paper, scissors, clear glue, fretsaw or craftknife, pins, card, poster paints, paintbrush.

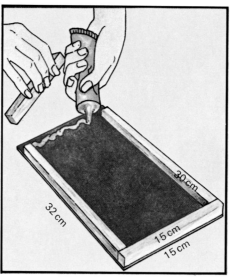

1. Measure a piece of card 32 cm × 15 cm, and cut. This will form the floor. Measure two pieces of balsa-wood 30 cm × 1 cm × 1 cm and two more 15 cm × 1 cm × 1 cm for the base, and cut. Glue in position.

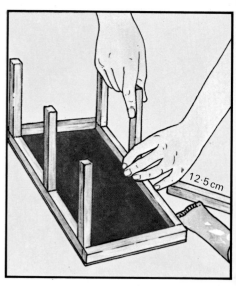

2. Measure and cut six pieces of wood 12·5 cm × 1 cm × 1 cm for the roof supports and glue each of them in place.

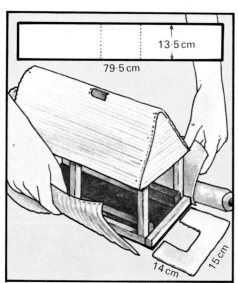

6. Use corrugated paper (or you may be able to get some artificial grass from a greengrocer) for the walls, measuring 79·5 cm × 13·5 cm (this will cover all three sides of the hall). Cut another piece of paper 15 cm × 14 cm for the doorway and make a hole for the opening. Glue into place.

7. Paint the roof to look like thatch (or green if you would like it to look like turf). The walls should be painted green. Leave to dry.

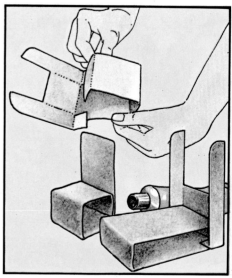

8. Furnish your Viking hall with a bed. Then make two chairs, one for the lord and the other for his lady. Place each one of these high chairs half-way along the sides of the hall.

9. A whole Viking settlement could be made if you add some smaller buildings to go beside your finished model of the hall.

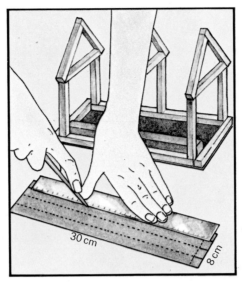

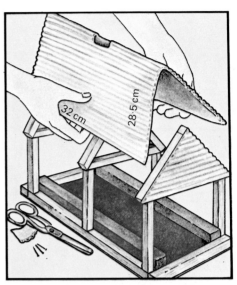

3. You will need three pieces of balsa-wood 12 cm, 13 cm and 16 cm × 1 cm × 1 cm, for each of the three rafter and crossbeam sections. Measure and cut as shown. Glue all three roof sections together and then glue these to the roof supports.

4. Make two benches from folded card each 30 cm × 8 cm. Paint and, when dry, glue into place along each side of the hall.

5. Cut a piece of corrugated paper 32 cm × 28·5 cm for the roof and make a smoke hole in the centre. Cut two triangles for each end of the roof to cover the end crossbeams and rafters, and glue these in place. Pin the main part of the roof in place so that you can lift it off.

More Unsolved Mysteries

There are many reasons why mysteries in archaeology exist. It may be that clues are hidden on a site, just waiting to be excavated. After much more research, for example, it may be possible to say exactly what happened to the Mayan, Indus and Minoan towns. On the other hand, information which was available in the past has often been destroyed, either by chance or on purpose, as when missionaries burnt the Mayan books, thinking that they were the work of devil worshippers. Occasionally, there is no real mystery at all. The mystery of Zimbabwe, for instance, was chiefly man-made. The early explorers wanted to believe that Zimbabwe was the site of the legendary King Solomon's Mines and ignored the evidence to the contrary. During the rest of this section, you can study brief accounts of five more mysteries.

Below: The great white horse of Westbury in southern England may have been the work of the Celtic people.

The Westbury Horse

Near the village of Bratton in Wiltshire a huge horse some 50 metres long has been carved out of the side of a chalk hill. There are carvings of other horses and a giant in the same area.

Why did the local people go to the trouble of carving this monstrous horse? According to local traditions, the Westbury Horse was created to commemorate Alfred the Great's victory over the Danes in A.D. 878. But, in that case, why did they not carve a horse and rider?

It is possible that the horse was made a great deal earlier by the Celts who ruled Britain until the time of the Roman conquest in A.D. 43. The Celts were particularly fond of their horses and often decorated their possessions with pictures of them. Moreover, the Westbury Horse is close to the site of an ancient Celtic camp.

Whoever the people were who produced the horse, they must have been considerable artists as the giant animal is accurately drawn.

Angkor Wat

About a century ago, Albert Henri Mouhot discovered the remains of a lost civilization in the jungles of Cambodia (modern Kampuchea). The most dazzling find was a series of 600 magnificent temples. The best preserved was Angkor Wat.

Archaeologists discovered that these temples were all that remained of the capital of the once mighty Khmer empire, which was founded in the ninth century A.D. and flourished for 500 years. At the height of their power the Khmers ruled much of what is now Thailand and Laos as well as Kampuchea. The Khmers' power was based on rice, the main product of their fertile, irrigated land. As their wealth grew, each successive king built finer and finer temples.

Why did the kings spend so much money in this way? French scholars believe that the kings' building obsession arose from a desire to gain and keep the favour of the gods. Each building marked the journey of the sun during the course of a year.

Mount Ararat

The story of Noah has always fascinated Jews, Christians and Moslems. According to the Bible, God warned Noah that a great flood was coming and ordered him to build an ark to contain two of every living thing. When the waters subsided, the ark came to rest on Mount Ararat.

By popular tradition, Mount Ararat is to be found in the Armenian Mountains in Turkey. Archaeologists have searched every centimetre of the 5000-metre-high mountain for signs of the ark. All they have found so far are bits of wood from trees that grow in the plains and not in the mountains.

However, as Sir Leonard Woolley proved, large-scale floods were fairly common in ancient Mesopotamia. He thought that the story of Noah probably referred to one of these.

Machu Picchu

In 1911, an American archaeologist called Hiram Bingham went to Peru in search of the legendary city of Vitcos, where the Incas under Manco made their last stand against the invading Spaniards in the 16th century. On attempting to retrace the steps of Manco, the last of the great Inca rulers, he discovered the ruins of a magnificent city about 2300 metres up in the Andes Mountains. This place is called Machu Picchu. Ruined walls and houses made of exquisitely cut square stones were found, as well as the remains of a royal burial place.

Was this Vitcos or some other Inca citadel? Bingham decided it was probably the city of Tampu Tocco, the original centre from where the Inca built up their great empire. Modern experts are divided over whether Machu Picchu was Tampu Tocco or some other Inca sanctuary.

The Soul Statues of Corsica

Single standing stones called *menhirs* have been found all over Europe including Corsica. In about 1500 B.C. the ancient Corsicans started to take much more care with these stones. Indeed, they became recognizable statues of warriors with crudely carved faces, tunics, swords and daggers.

Why did this sudden change take place? Between the 14th and 12th centuries B.C., bands of warriors invaded many of the lands of the eastern Mediterranean. A French archaeologist called Roger Grosjean believes that the ancient Corsicans carved statues of the invading chiefs whom they had killed in battle. Why did they do this?

Perhaps they hoped that the spirits of these chiefs, who possessed superior weapons, would live on in the statues and frighten away and beat off the attacks of further invaders. If this is so, they were mistaken, because the invaders drove the Corsicans from their island and took their place.

Above: The remote city of Machu Picchu may have been the last stronghold of the Incas.

Below: Corsica, off the west coast of Italy, is the site of many strange statues like these.

75

Glossary

Amphora (pl. amphorae): a large double-handled, narrow-necked, storage jar.

Archaeology: the study of man-made objects and ruins, usually dating from the ancient past.

Artefact: any kind of man-made object.

Balsa-wood: light, strong wood from the American balsa tree.

Barbarian: a foreigner or uncultured person, especially in ancient history; also used specifically to describe someone outside the Roman Empire or a non-Christian.

Bluestone: stone (so-called because of its colour) mined in the Prescelly Mountains in south-west Wales; also one of the columns shaped from this stone and transported to Stonehenge by prehistoric peoples.

Bog: wet spongy soil containing decaying and decayed moss and other vegetable matter which helps to preserve organic materials deposited in it.

Celt: a prehistoric people who invaded Britain at the end of the fifth century B.C. and remained in control until the British were conquered by the Romans in the year A.D. 43.

76

Citadel: a stronghold or a particularly strongly fortified place in a town, often situated on a hill.

Civilization: a form of advanced urban life involving a dense population, the erection of monumental buildings, the development of a class structure, trade, organized religion, recording systems (reading, writing and arithmetic), and craft specialization.

Codex (pl. codices): ancient manuscript text, especially Mexican, usually about a king.

Dialogue: a conversation and, in the case of Plato's dialogues, a way of resolving a problem with a series of questions and answers.

Druid: one of an order of priests of the Celts in France and Britain from at least the first century B.C. to the first century A.D.

Excavate: uncover an ancient site in a specially planned and scientific way to obtain as much information from the site as possible.

Fossil: an organic remain which has been preserved in soil, rocks, bogs, and so on.

Fresco: a type of water-colour picture painted on a wall covered in fresh plaster or damp mortar.

Glyph: an ancient sculptured character or symbol inscription.

Guano: birds' droppings which form a rich manure, found in quantity on islands near Peru.

Halberd: a combined spear and battle-axe.

Hieroglyph: a figure of an object standing for a word or part of a word as used in ancient Egyptian writing.

Iron Age: a period of prehistory when iron replaced bronze or some other metal as the most important material from which weapons, armour, and other technological items were made.

Irrigation: way of watering land using network of ditches.

Lintel: a horizontal beam or stone joining uprights, as in the case of a door or window.

Longship: a long, narrow, shallow-drafted, one-masted, sail- or oar-propelled Viking warship.

Menhir: a single plain or sculptured upright standing stone.

Middle Ages: the period of history between about 410 and 1450.

Mummified: used to describe a corpse preserved by exposure to a dry atmosphere (see page 65), or one preserved with spices and chemicals, as in ancient Egypt.

Mycenaean: an inhabitant of the Bronze Age city of Mycenae in southern Greece.

Old World: the countries of the Eastern hemisphere (i.e. all those excluding the Americas).

Prehistoric: the word used to describe the period before written history.

Primate: the highest order of mammals including man, apes, tarsiers and lemurs.

Quartzite: a metamorphic rock, formed by intense heat or pressure, consisting of grains of sandstone surrounded with a deposit of quartz.

Radio-carbon dating: a method of dating organic materials by establishing the amount of carbon 14 present in them: during life, materials absorb carbon 14 from the atmosphere and, during decay, the carbon 14 content lessens. This dating system is not exact as the amount of carbon 14 in the atmosphere has varied. Firm radio-carbon dates were not possible until an age sequence of bristlecone pine tree-rings was established and the carbon 14 content of each ring was measured. It is now possible to give absolute dates for objects whose carbon 14 date can be compared with the bristlecone pine sequence.

Rune (adj. runic): a letter in a form of writing carved on wood or stone by ancient peoples, including the Vikings.

Saga: a medieval Icelandic or Norwegian story, especially one telling the history of a family or royal person.

Sarsen: a natural sandstone which occurs as huge boulders on the surface of the Marlborough Downs; also one of the columns quarried from this sandstone and hauled 20 miles to Stonehenge by prehistoric peoples.

Sauna: a bath in steam from water that has been thrown on to heated stones, or the building for this bath, used since Viking days.

Site: an area where ancient ruins and/or artefacts have been discovered.

Slash-and-burn agriculture: the first European farmers cut down the forests (slash), set fire to the fallen trees (burn) and sowed their plants in the rich ashes (agriculture).

Soapstone: see steatite.

Steatite (soapstone): a rock which is easy to carve and can be made into many kinds of ornament and items such as bowls and vases.

Stele (pl. stelae): an upright stone column or slab, decorated with carvings and/or inscriptions.

Stone Age: a period of prehistory earlier than the Iron and Bronze Ages, when stone was the most important material for making weapons and other implements.

Terrace: a flat surface cut into the side of a hill or mountain to form a field, surrounded with walls to retain the soil and water.

Tidal wave: a huge wave caused by an earthquake or volcanic eruption.

Trilithon: a stone arch made up of two uprights supporting a lintel.

Ziggurat: a rectangular temple constructed in tiers which was originated by the ancient peoples of Mesopotamia (modern Iraq), whose last capital was Babylon.

Index
Bold face indicates pages on which illustrations appear.

Abominable Snowman 17
Agriculture, among Maya 38, 40–1
  among Nazca 62
  in Indus Valley 28–9
Alfred the Great 74
Amnissos 11
Amyitis 32
Angkor Wat 74
Antillia 10
Apes, giant **14–15**
Ararat, Mt 74
Ariadne 44, 47
Arthur, King 12
Aryans 29
Ascension Island 11
Assyria 32, 35
Atalante 11
Athens 44
Atlantis 8–11, 28
Atlas 8
Avalon 12
Avon, River 20, 23
Azores 11

Babylon 32–6
Bantu 53
Bigfoot 17
Bilaspur 16
Bjaeldskov Valley 58
Bluestones 20, **25**

Cahuachi 62
Cambodia 74
Canada 71
Celts 22, 23, 74
China 14, 16–17
Clito 8
Codices, Mayan 38, 40, **41, 42–3**
Columbus, Christopher 10, 71
Copenhagen 59
Corsica 75
Crete 11, 44, 46–7
Critias (Plato) 10
Cuzco 65
Cyrus 32

Da Gama, Vasco 10
Daedalus 48
De Landa, Bishop 40
Denmark 58–9
Dresden Codex **41, 42**
Druids **22**, 23
Dryopithecus 17

Easter Island 6–7
Eclipses 23
Egypt 28, 32, 48, 53
Eriksson, Leif 68
Evans, Sir Arthur **46**, 47

Fort Victoria 52
Fossils 16, 17
Freydis 68
Frome, River 20

Giants 16–17
Giganthropus 16
Gigantopithecus 16, 17, 18
Glyphs 39, **41, 42–3**
Greeks, Ancient 10, 11, 23, 44, 46, 47
Greenland 70, 71, 72
Guadalquivir River 11
Guatemala 40

Hanging Gardens of Babylon 32–6
Heyerdahl, Thor 7
Hong Kong 16

Iceland 70, 72
Incas 65, 75
India 10, 16, 53
Indus Valley, 26, 28–9
Ingstad, Helge 71, 72
Iraq 34
Ishtar Gate **33, 34**, 35

Java Man 16
Jerusalem 32, 53
Jutland 56

Kampuchea 74
Karlsefni, Thorfinn 68
Kensington, Minnesota 70
Khmer Empire 74
Knossos 46, **47–8**
Koldewey, Robert 34, 35, 36
Kosok, Paul 64
Kwangsi Province 16, 17

L'Anse-aux-Meadows 70, 71, 72
Labrador 71
Lintels 20
Longships 68

Machu Picchu **75**

Maize 38, 40
Marduk 32, 34, 35
Marduk-apal-iddin 35
Marlborough Downs 20
Mauch, Karl 52, 53
Maudslay, Alfred 40
Maya 38–43, 74
Medes & Persians 32
Menhirs 75
Milpas 40
Minoan civilization 10, 11, 44–9
Minos 44, 46, 47
Minotaur 44, **45**, 47
Mohenjo-daro **26–7**, 28–9, 30
Monomotapa 50, 53
Mozambique 53
Mycenaeans 23

Nabu 34
Nazca 62–6
Nebuchadnezzar 32, 35
Newfoundland 68
Nigeria 10
Nipigon, Lake 70
Noah 74
Northwest River 71

Ohman, Olaf 70

Pakistan 26–30
Palestine 11, 53
Pei, Professor W. C. 16
Peking Man 16
Peru 7, 10, 64–5, 75
Petén 38
Phoenicians 11, 53
Pitcairn Island 7
Plato 10, 11, 28
Polynesia 7
Poseidon 8
Prescelly Mts 20

Radio-carbon dating 23, 24, 53, 71
Randall-MacIver, David 53
Rigveda 29
Rio Grande 64
Roussel, Aage 71

Sagas 70, 71
Salisbury Plain 20, 22, 23, 24
Sandnes 71

Santorini 10
Sarsens 20, 23, 24, **25**
Sasquatch 17
Schliemann, Heinrich 10
Schliemann, Paul 10
Severn Estuary 20
Sheba, Queen of 50, 53
Siwalik Hills 16
Skraelings 68
Soapstone (steatite) 47, 52, 53
Socrates 10
Sofala 50
Solomon, King 50, 53, 74
Spence, Lewis 10, 11
Stonehenge 20–1, 22–3, 24
Sumeria 28

Tampu Tocco 75
Tartessos 11
Teeth, primates' 16, **17**, **18**
Thailand 74
Theseus 44, 46, 47
Tikal 38–9, **40**, 41
Timaeus (Plato) 10
Tollund Fen 56, 58–9
Tower of Babel 35
Trilithons 20, **25**
Tristan da Cunha 11
Troy 10
Turkey 74
Tyre 11, 53

Vikings 68–72
Vinland 68, 70–1
Vinland Map **70–1**
Vitcos 75
Von Koenigswald, G. H. R. 16, 17

Wales 12, 20
Watussi tribe 18
Weidenrich, Professor 18
West Indies 10
Westbury Horse **74**
Wheeler, Sir Mortimer 59
Woolley, Sir Leonard 74
Wylye, River 20

Zaire 18, 53
Ziggurat 35
Zimbabwe 50–4, 74
Zimbabwe-Rhodesia 52